Building with Butterflies

How to build stunning sculptures from simple units made by folding paper

David Mitchell

2nd Edition

Revised and expanded 2011

A Water Trade publication
www.watertradebooks.co.uk

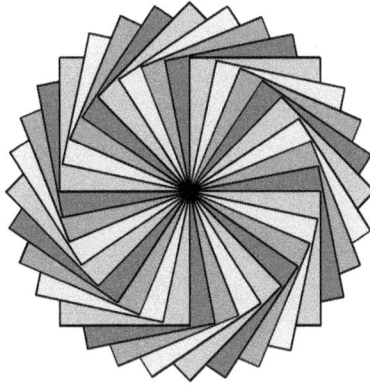

About Water Trade

Water Trade is a micro-publisher of books about aspects of origami and paperfolding. We aim to publish books containing original material of the highest quality organised around technically interesting or unusual themes, and which are consequently far more than simply collections of instructions for designs. We welcome submissions from new or established authors on potential themes for future books.

About David Mitchell

David Mitchell has been a professional author, illustrator and designer specialising in origami for many years. He lives in Kendal, close to the mountains of the English Lake District, where he loves to walk. He is also a passionate fan of latin dance and music, particularly salsa and bachata.

As a designer he is particularly well known for his innovative modular and macro-modular sculptures but is also a prolific inventor of single and multi-piece paperfolds, action novelties and puzzles.

His other books include Complete Origami, Mathematical Origami, The Magic of Flexagons, Paper Crystals, Origami Animals, Paperfolding Puzzles, Origami Alfresco, Paper Planes, and Sticky Note Origami.

David Mitchell can be contacted through his website www.origamiheaven.com

Contents

Introduction   6
How to understand the folding
instructions   8

A Homage to Paul Jackson's Cube

Paul Jackson's Cube   12

Pattern Variations

Iso Cubes   18
The Chequerboard Cube   21
Yin Yang Cubes   25
Single Diagonal Stripe Cubes   31
Double Diagonal Stripe Cubes   36

Distortions

The Columbus Cube   42
The Tetracube   44
The Paul Jackson Cuboctahedron   46
Metamorphosis   49
Metamorphosis 2   53
The Icarus Cube   55

The Sculptures

The Columbus Tower   60
The Columbus Pyramid   61
The Columbus Tower Revisited   67
Ring of Cubes   68
Ball of Cubes   71
The Icarus Tower   73

Building with Butterflies

The Modules

The Alpha module   80
The Beta module   81

The Gamma module   82
The Delta module   83
The Epsilon module   84
The Zeta module   85

The Assemblies

The Alpha Prism   88
The Twin Prisms   89
The Alpha Cuboctahedron   90
The Beta Prism   91
The Diamond Prism   92
The Gamma Antiprism   94
Robert Neale's Octahedron   95
The Rosebud Octahedron   96
The Hybrid Prism   98
The Epsilon Star   99
The Zeta Hexahedron   100

The Sculptures

Alpha Pyramids   102
Damocles   106
Treesnake   109
Helterskelter   111
The Octahedral Tower   112
The Octahedral Pyramid   113

Combination Sculptures

The Crooked Tower   120
Tricorne   121
The Leaning Tower   124
Slide   125

And Finally

Tokyo Towers   130

Introduction

This book contains details of two explorations in modular origami design, Building with Butterflies itself and A Homage to Paul Jackson's Cube. Both explorations start from a very simple beginning and end up in quite surprising places. They also interconnect, which provides a rather neat rationale for the inclusion of both in the same book.

Although I discovered all the designs explained in this book for myself, I subsequently found that some of them had previously been discovered by other paperfolders. The designs this applies to are Robert Neale's Octahedron, Paul Jackson's Cube and Cuboctahedron and Kenneth Kawamura's Butterfly Ball (which I call the Alpha Cuboctahedron). The design I call the Epsilon Star was also quite independently discovered by both Kenneth Kawamura and Robert Neale, though I have been unable to determine who has priority. Kenneth Kawamura calls it the Harlequin Star and Robert Neale the Blue Balloon. Such multiple discovery was common in the early days of the exploration of the possibilities inherent in modular origami design when designers largely worked in isolation from each other. There was no internet in those days, of course.

The starting point of the Building with Butterflies exploration is a group of closely related modules of a very basic design. These are the butterflies of the title. It turns out that these modules can be woven together in a compact manner to produce a range of modular assemblies. Some of these assemblies, such as the Diamond Prism, the Hybrid Prism and the Epsilon Star are very delicate (and consequently quite challenging to assemble). Others, such as Robert Neale's Octahedron are surprisingly robust. Most are somewhere in between.

The Alpha Cuboctahedron, the Gamma Antiprism and the Epsilon Star are examples of even distribution designs, which is to say that the paper is evenly distributed over the surface of the form (so that every part of the design is made from the same number of layers of paper, in this case two). Robert Neale's Octahedron also possesses this property, although there is no space between the opposite outside surfaces. The distribution of the paper in the other assemblies is less even. This is because, even though the modules themselves do not have tabs or pockets of their own, it is possible to weave modules together to form sub-assemblies which do.

While pursuing this exploration, I found that it was possible to combine many of these modular designs into second generation assemblies. There did not seem to be a word for such second generation assemblies so, in order to make them easier to talk about, I invented one. I call them macro-modular assemblies or sculptures and, in this context, I call the first generation designs they are built from macro-modules.

Macro-modules built from butterfly modules can be combined in several ways. The simplest way to combine them is simply to stack them on top of each other to form towers. Stacking Gamma Antiprisms, for instance, is sufficient by itself to create the sculpture I call Helterskelter (because of the way the ridges of the macro-modules spiral around the form). This is a big result from a very simple idea.

It was then relatively straightforward to design link units (modules that link or separate elements of a macro-modular structure but are not inserted into pockets) to turn these basic towers into pyramids. I also found that it was possible to create sculptures by turning some of the pockets of their constituent sub-assemblies into tabs (or by leaving the pockets alone and designing joining pieces to do the same job).

The final insight was that it is possible to create more complex sculptures still by combining macro-modular assemblies. The results of doing this with Alpha Pyramids are shown on page 105. So far I have been able to resist inventing a new word for this type of structure.

The starting point of the other exploration, A Homage to Paul Jackson's Cube, is, of course, the cube this title refers to, which is possibly the best design in the whole of the modular origami repertoire. This is also an example of an even distribution design, although, once assembled, it is twice as thick, four layers deep, at every point. The modules are not provided with pockets, although they do have tabs, which go inside the design. Because the gaps between the tabs along the open edges of the modules are slightly less wide than the tabs themselves (which is due to the thickness of the paper) friction between the modules (or perhaps a slight mutual inwards pressure) acts to keep the modules locked together. The finished cube is a surprisingly strong construction and can easily withstand being thrown around.

This exploration first looks at ways to pattern the surface of Paul Jackson's Cube, then at ways to distort the surface, by inverting the corners and bringing out the centre of the faces. Finally it looks at how some of these distortions (along with the original unaltered cube itself) can be utilised as macro-modules to create sculptures in the form of towers, pyramids, rings and balls.

The biggest surprise of this exploration was the effect of altering the modules to pattern the surface of the cube. Unexpectedly, I found that in many cases the modules could be taken apart and reassembled to produce dramatically different results. It is a neat piece of serendipity (for which I am happy to claim full credit) that Paul Jackson's Cube is almost unique among modular designs in the ease with which this taking apart and reassembly can be achieved.

Finally, even though it is a multi-piece rather than a modular design, I have chosen to include the Tokyo Towers in this book, on the basis that the sculptures are of an essentially similar kind. I hope you will enjoy the challenge of building them.

David Mitchell

How to understand the folding instructions

The edges of the paper are shown as solid lines.

Each picture is numbered. You should be careful to read them in the correct order.

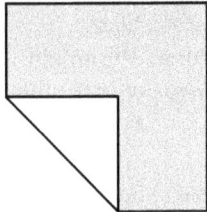

Shading is used to show which side of the paper is coloured.

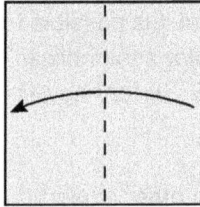

A folding instruction consists of a movement arrow, a fold line and a written explanation that may contain information not shown in the picture.

1. Fold in half sideways.

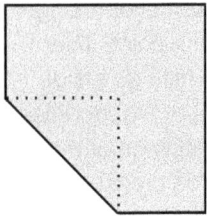

Dotted lines are used to show hidden edges and fold lines or imaginary lines that are used to help locate a fold.

A movement arrow shows you which part of the paper moves and where it goes to.

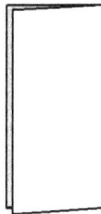

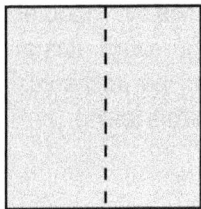

This is the result of following the instruction above. Edges which lie exactly on top of each other as the result of a fold are sometimes shown slightly offset on the after diagram.

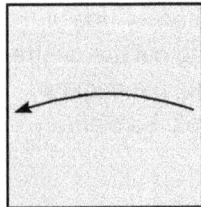

A fold line shows you where the new crease will form when you flatten the fold. A dashed fold line means the fold is made towards you. You should always flatten the fold unless you are told not to.

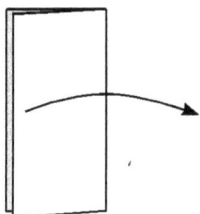

A movement arrow without a fold line means unfold in the direction indicated.

This picture also shows you how a single picture can show you the result of making the previous fold as well as how to make the next one.

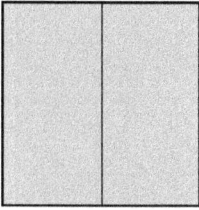

Creases you have already made are shown as thin lines.

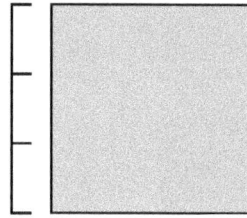

The ruler symbol shows that the adjacent edge should be seen as divided into a number of equal sections.

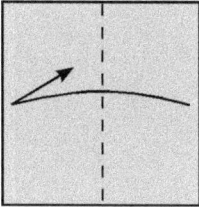

This version of the movement arrow means fold, crease, then unfold.

This symbol tells you to apply gentle pressure to the paper in the direction the arrowhead is pointing.

A dashed and dotted fold line means that the fold should be made away from you.

This arrow tells you to pull some part of the paper gently in the direction the arrow is pointing.

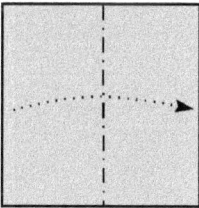

The movement arrow that goes with this picture is shown with a dotted shaft because the fold is made behind the paper.

This symbol tells you to turn the paper over. The written instruction will tell you in which direction.

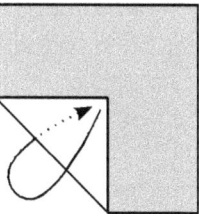

A circle is used to draw attention to some particular part of a picture referred to in a written explanation.

This picture tells you to swing the flap backwards out of sight by reversing the direction of the existing crease.

This symbol tells you that the next diagram has been drawn on a larger scale.

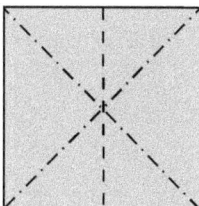

A combination of fold lines show you how the paper can be collapsed into a different shape.

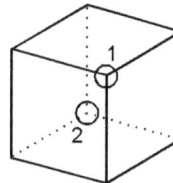

This symbol is used to show you the relationship between two views of the same cube. In the second view the corner marked 2 will have been rotated to position 1.

9

A Homage to
Paul Jackson's Cube

Paul Jackson's Cube

You will need six square sheets of paper. Paul Jackson's Cube is a very versatile design and almost any kind of paper will do. If you are using irogami (paper that is white on one surface and coloured on the other) begin with your paper arranged white side up.

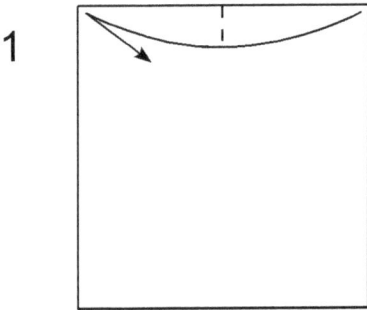

1

1. Make a tiny crease to mark the middle of the top edge.

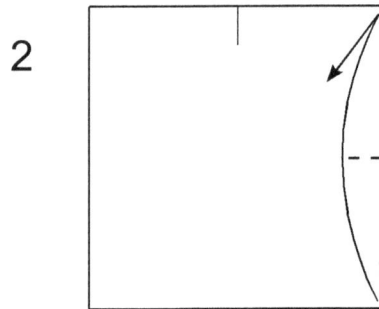

2

2. Mark the middle of the right hand edge in a similar way.

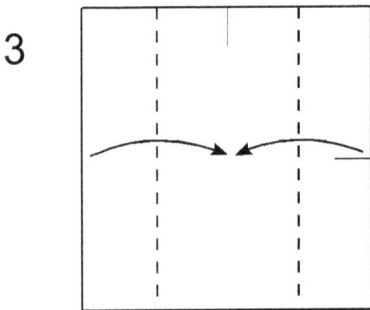

3

3. Fold both outside edges to the centre using the crease you made in step 1 as a guide.

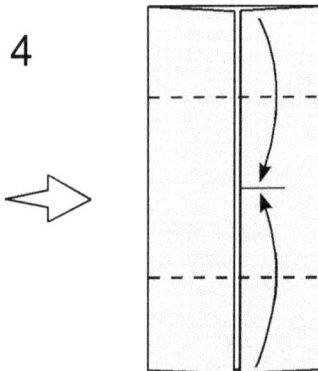

4

4. Fold the top and bottom edges to the centre using the crease you made in step 2 as a guide.

David Mitchell / Building with Butterflies

5

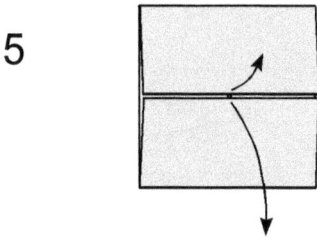

5. Open up both tabs at right angles.

6

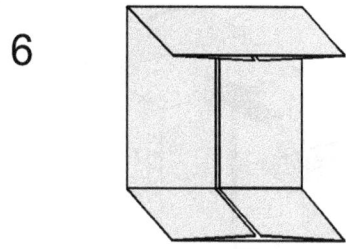

6. This is the standard module.

7

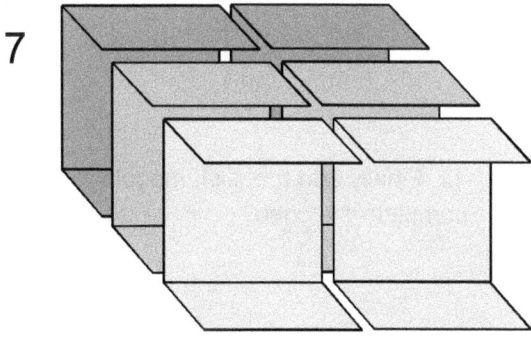

7. You need six standard modules to make Paul Jackson's Cube.

8

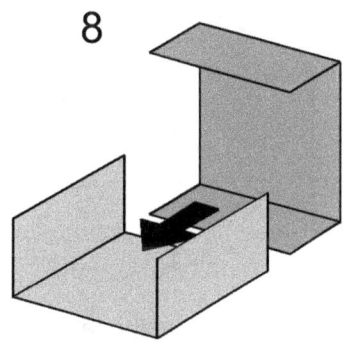

8. Slide the bottom tab of one module into the open edge of another.

9

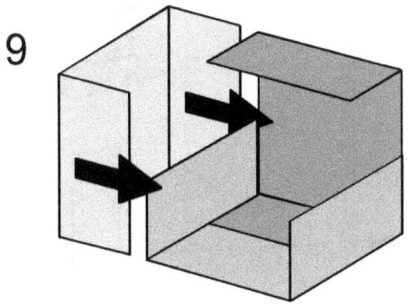

9. Add the third module to complete one corner ...

10

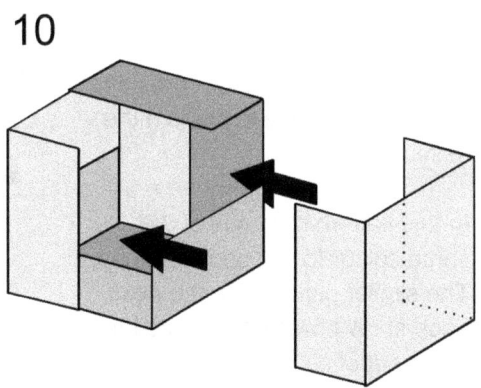

10. ... then add the fourth module like this.

11

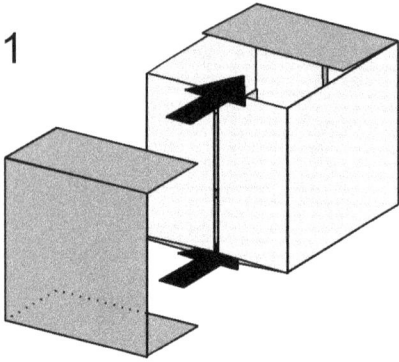

11. The fifth module slides in like this.

12

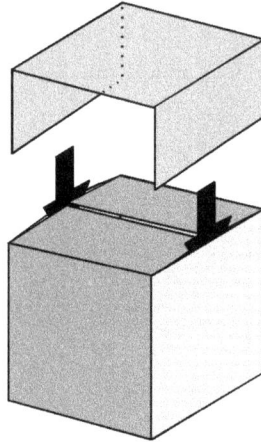

12. Finally add the sixth module to complete the cube.

13

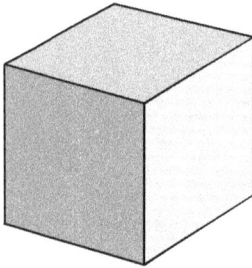

13. Check that none of the tabs are visible. Paul Jackson's Cube is finished. If you have folded your modules accurately the cube will lock solidly together.

14. This type of diagram provides an alternative way to explain the assembly process.

In this pattern modules of the same colour form opposite faces. The similar pictures on the next page show how to assemble the same set of six modules (consisting of two modules in each of three colours) into cubes which are patterned in other ways.

14

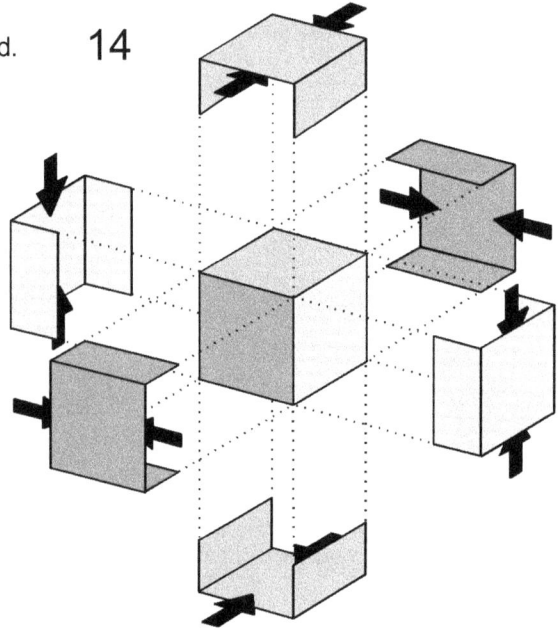

15

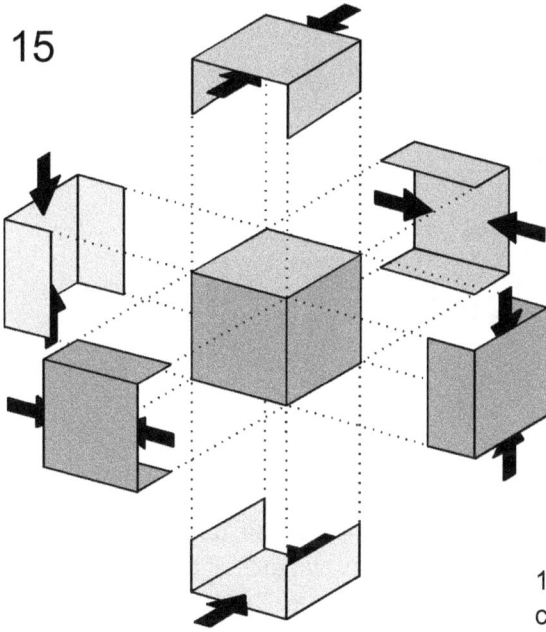

15. In this pattern modules of the same colour form adjoining faces.

16

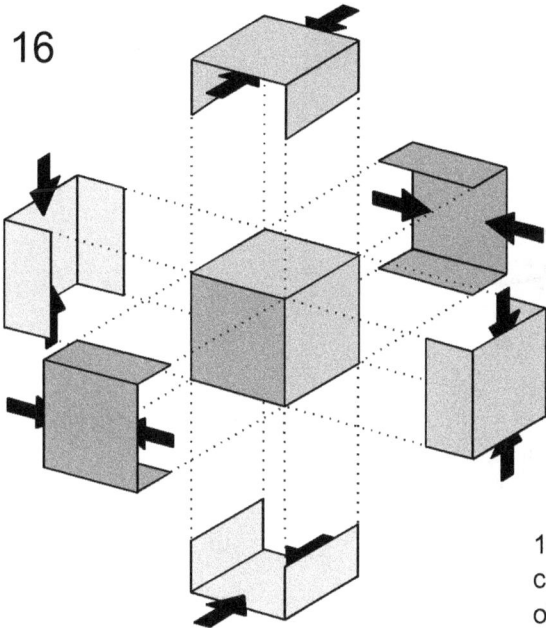

16. In this pattern the modules of one colour form opposite faces while the other two pairs form adjoining faces.

17

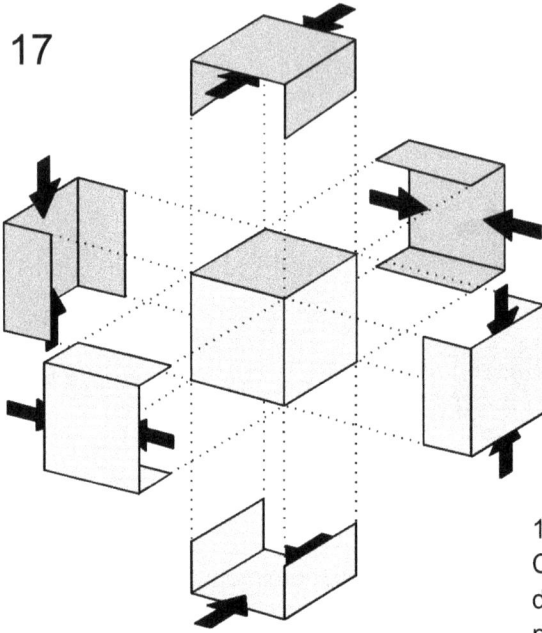

17. You can also make Paul Jackson's Cube using two sets of three modules of different colours. Two arrangements are possible. This one ...

18

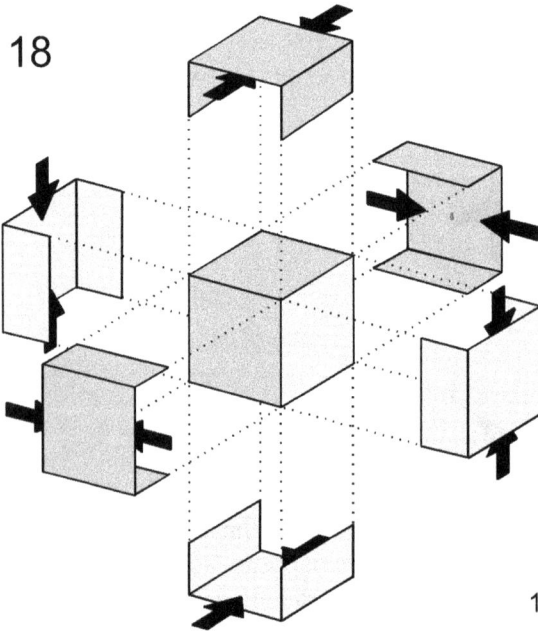

18. ... and this one.

A Homage to Paul Jackson's Cube

Pattern Variations

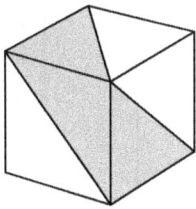 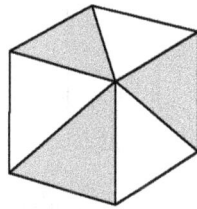

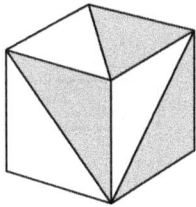 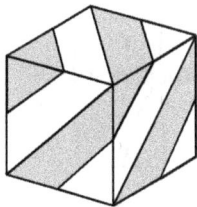

Iso Cubes

Iso Cubes are the simplest pattern variation of Paul Jackson's Cube but they are not without interest.

You will need six square sheets of irogami to make an Iso Cube. Begin by following steps 1 to 3 of Paul Jackson's Cube (see page 12).

4

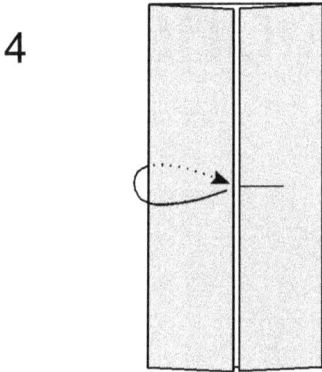

4. Swing the left hand flap out of sight behind using the existing crease.

5

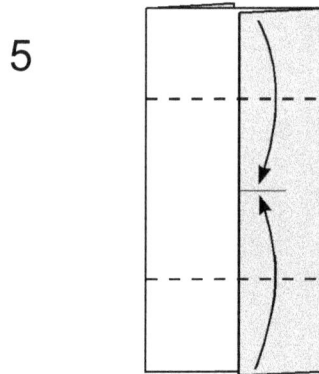

5. Fold the top and bottom edges into the centre using the crease made in step 2 as a guide.

6

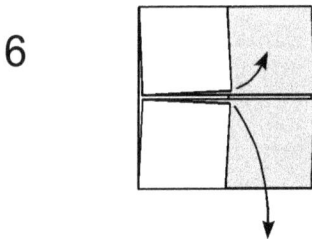

6. Open out both tabs at right angles.

7

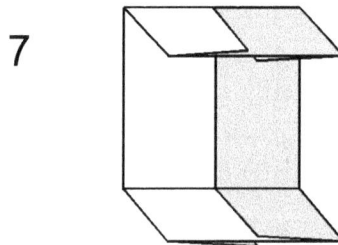

7. Make six identical modules.

8

9

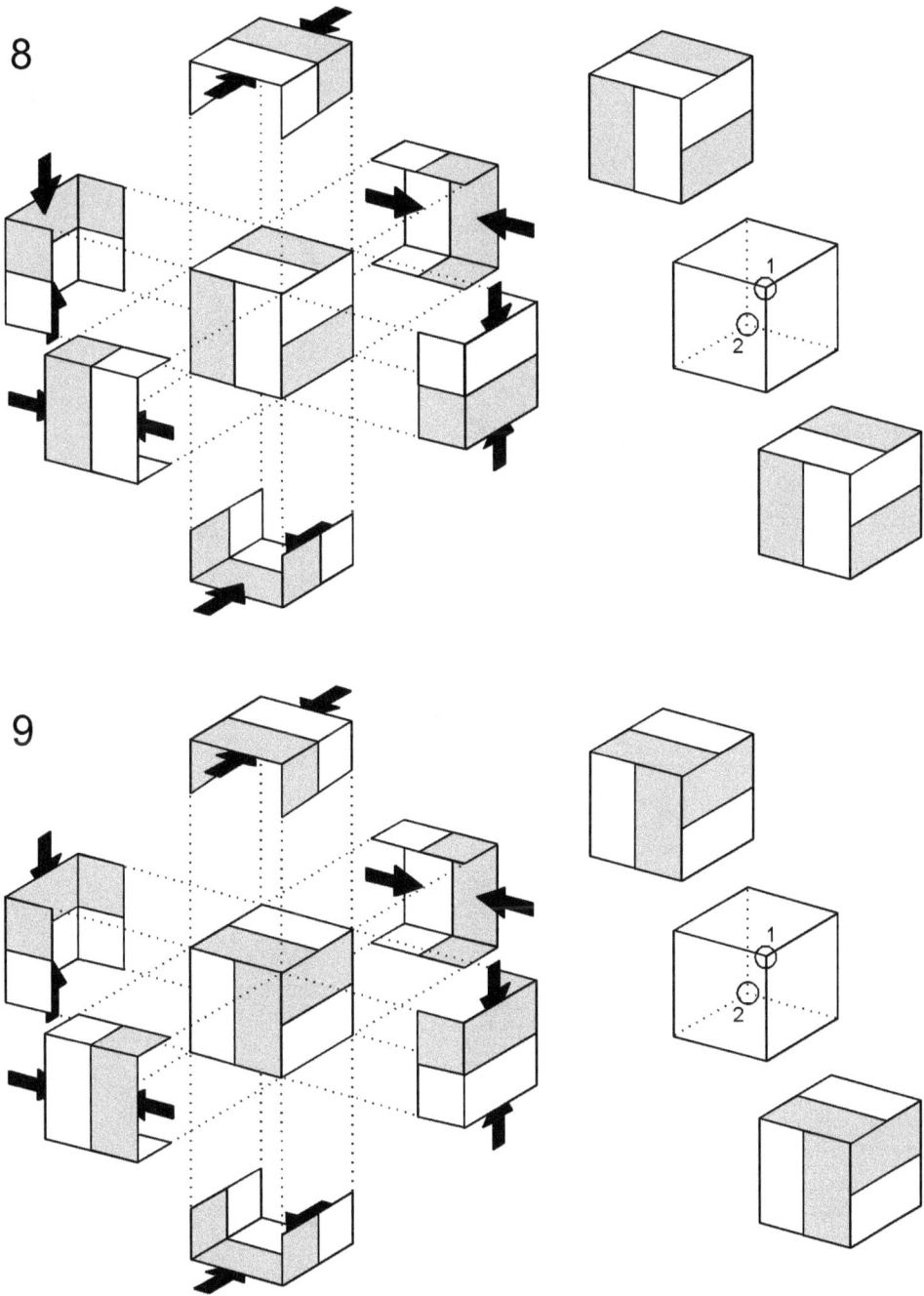

8 and 9. The two cubes shown above are negatives of each other. Although you cannot see it in these pictures, in both cases the colour at the perimeter of the visible faces forms a continuous band around all the faces of the cube.

10

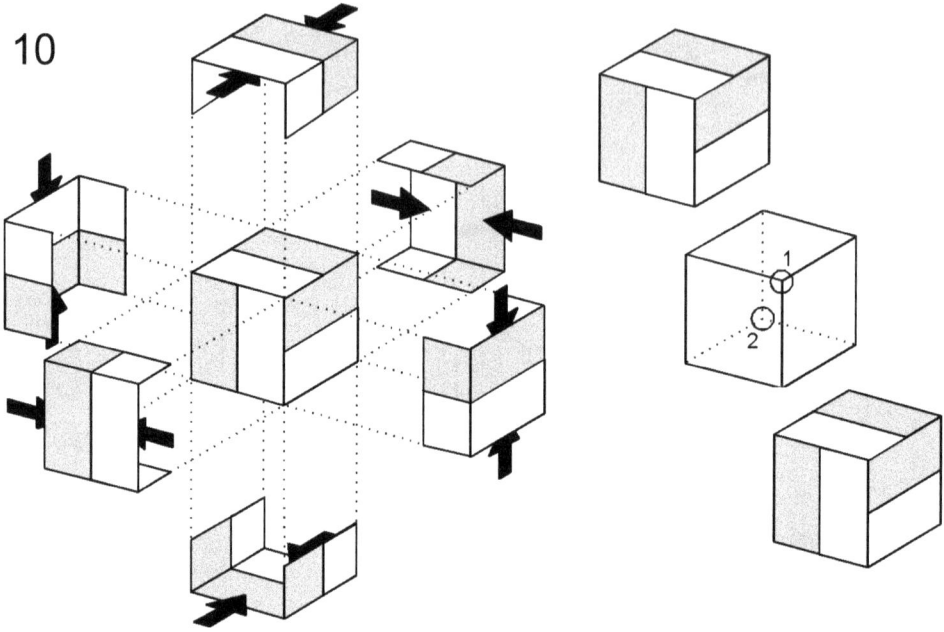

10. The cubes shown in pictures 8 and 9 can be converted into each other just by rearranging two opposite modules. To see how this is done compare this picture with picture 8.

11

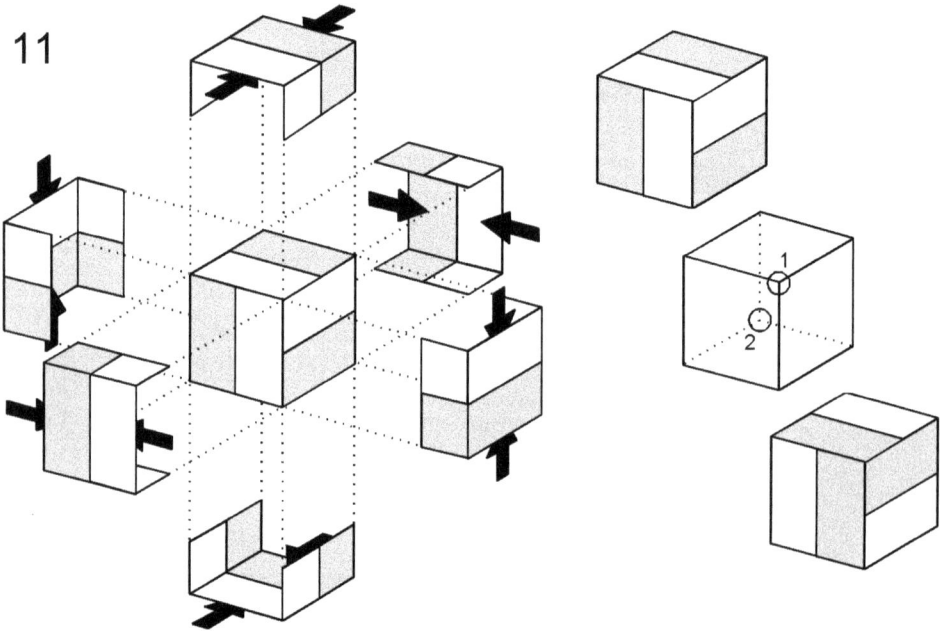

11. This arrangement produces a cube with a negative pattern on opposite corners.

The Chequerboard Cube

Each face of the Chequerboard Cube is patterned like a small section of a chessboard. To achieve a module to create this cube it is first necessary to divide the paper into a 3x3 grid of smaller squares.

You will need six squares of irogami for the cube and another square of the same size to use as a template.

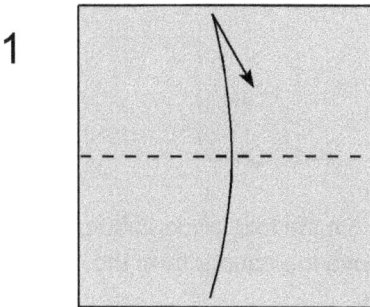

1

1. Fold the template in half upwards, then unfold.

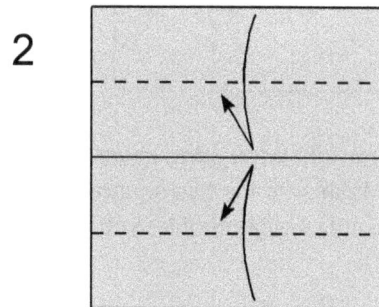

2

2. Fold the top and bottom edges to the centre, then unfold.

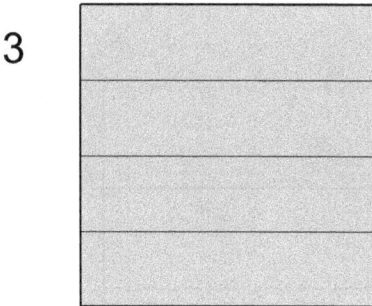

3

3. The template is finished.

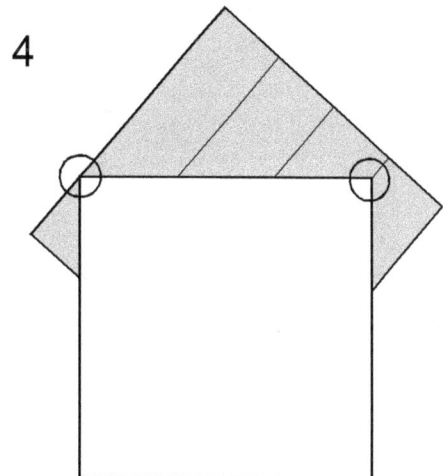

4

4. Lay your paper in front of the template white side up and carefully align the top corners like this.

5

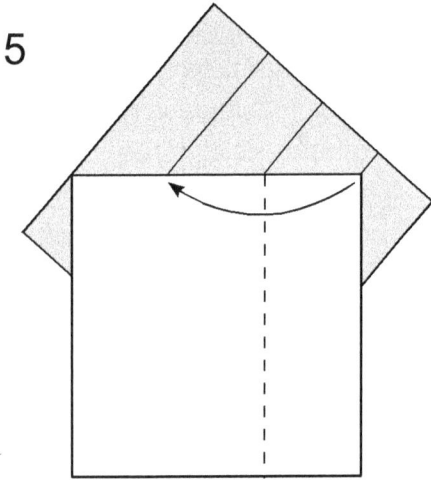

5. Fold the right hand edge inwards as shown. Make sure the two squares don't slip out of alignment as you make this fold.

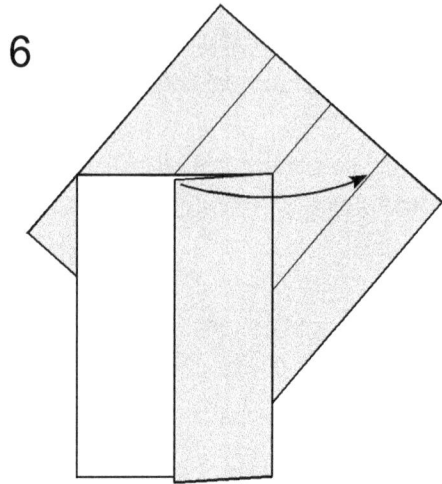

6

6. Open out the fold made in step 5 and remove the square from the template.

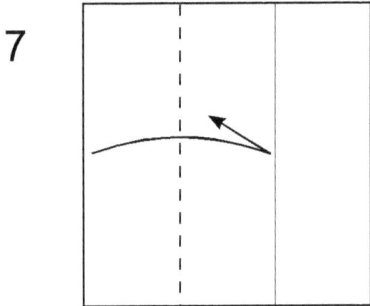

7

7. Fold the left hand edge onto the crease made in step 5, crease, then unfold.

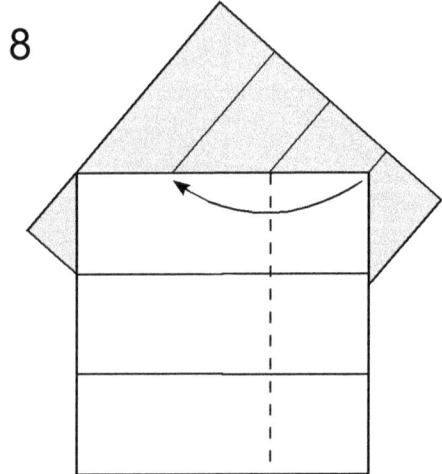

8

8. Your paper is now divided into thirds. To divide the paper into thirds in the other direction as well, rotate the square through ninety degrees and repeat steps 4 to 7.

9

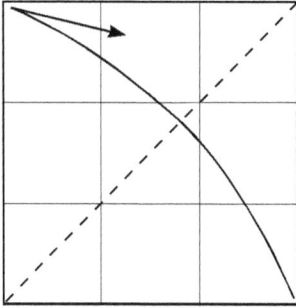

9. This is the result. The paper is now divided into nine smaller squares. Fold in half diagonally, then unfold.

10

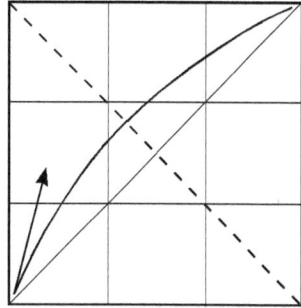

10. Fold in half diagonally in the opposite direction, then unfold.

11

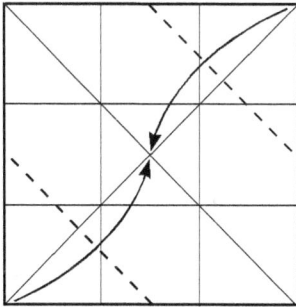

11. Fold two opposite corners into the centre.

12

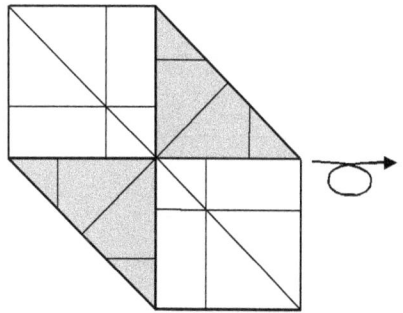

12. Turn over sideways.

13

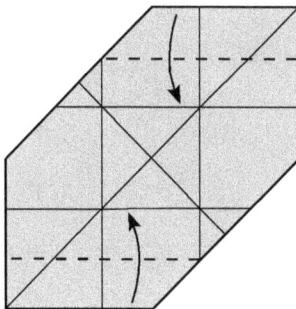

13. Fold the top and bottom edges inwards as shown.

14

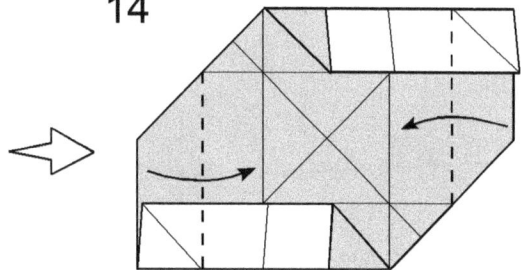

14. Fold the left and right hand edges inwards in a similar way.

15

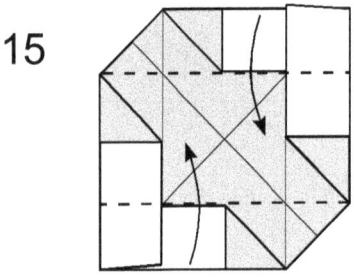

15. Fold the top and bottom edges inwards again along the line of the existing creases.

16

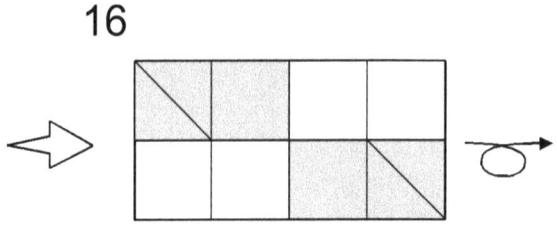

16. Turn over sideways.

17

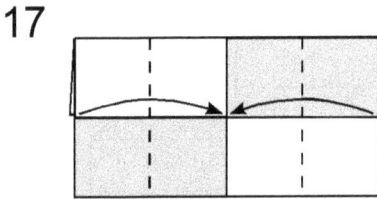

17. Fold the left and right edges inwards along the line of the existing creases.

18

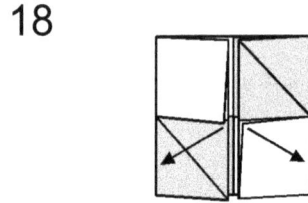

18. Open up both tabs at right angles.

19

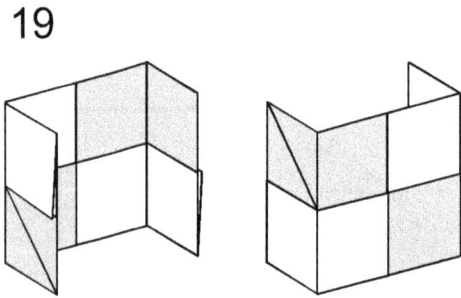

19. Make six identical modules and assemble in the same way as Paul Jackson's Cube (see pages 13 and 14).

20

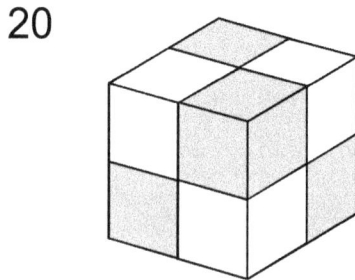

20. The Chequerboard Cube is finished.

Yin Yang Cubes

The faces of Yin Yang Cubes are divided diagonally rather than vertically or horizontally. This allows the creation of mirror-image modules, with curious results.

You will need six squares of irogami. Begin by following steps 1 to 8 of the Chequerboard Cube (see page 21). Yin Yang modules can also be made by following the same folding sequence but beginning coloured side up.

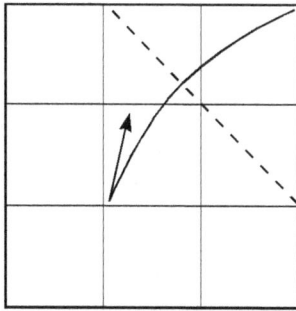

9. Fold the top right corner diagonally inwards as shown, then unfold.

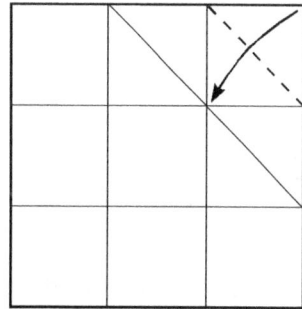

10. Fold the top right corner diagonally inwards again.

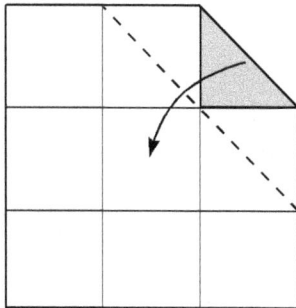

11. Remake fold 9.

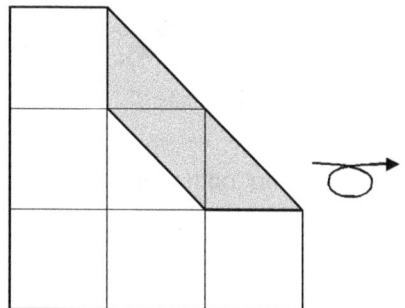

12. Turn over sideways.

13

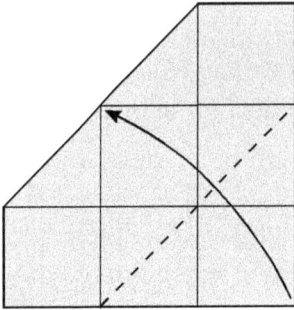

13. Fold the bottom right corner diagonally inwards.

14

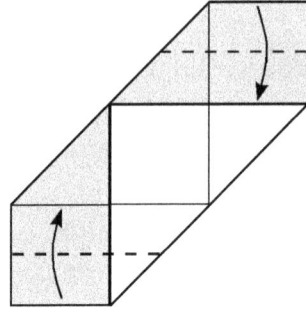

14. Fold the top and bottom edges inwards.

15

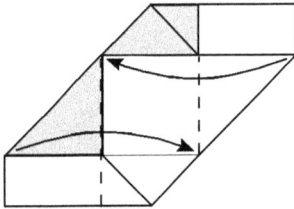

15. Fold the left and right hand edges inwards using the existing creases.

16

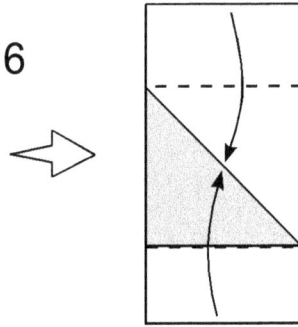

16. Fold the top and bottom edges to the centre using the existing creases.

17

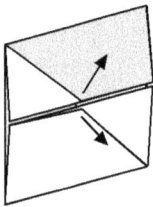

17. Open out both tabs at right angles.

18

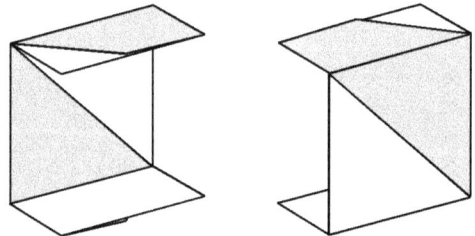

18. Make six identical modules.

19

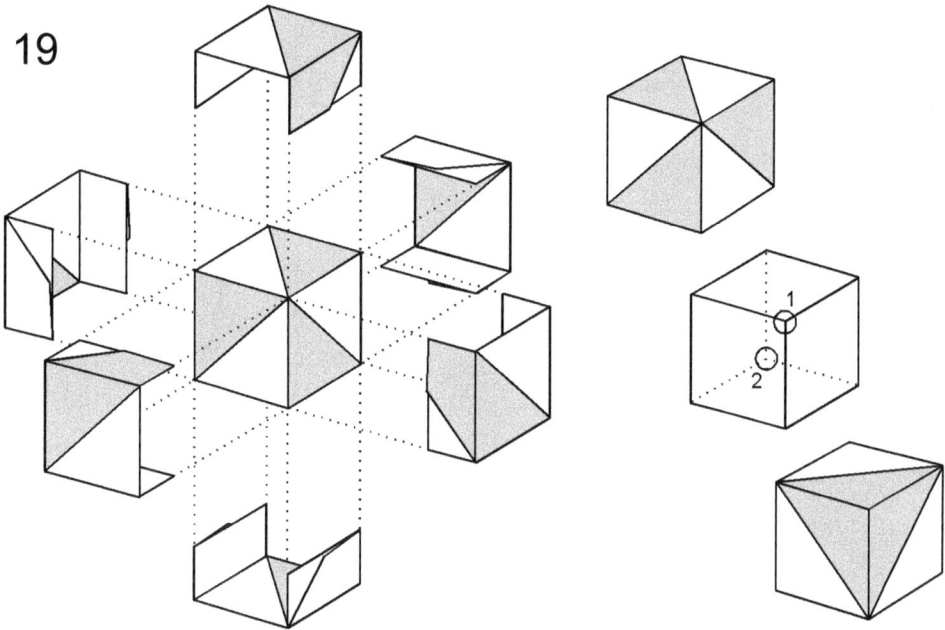

19. Putting the modules together like this will produce the cube shown on the right.

20

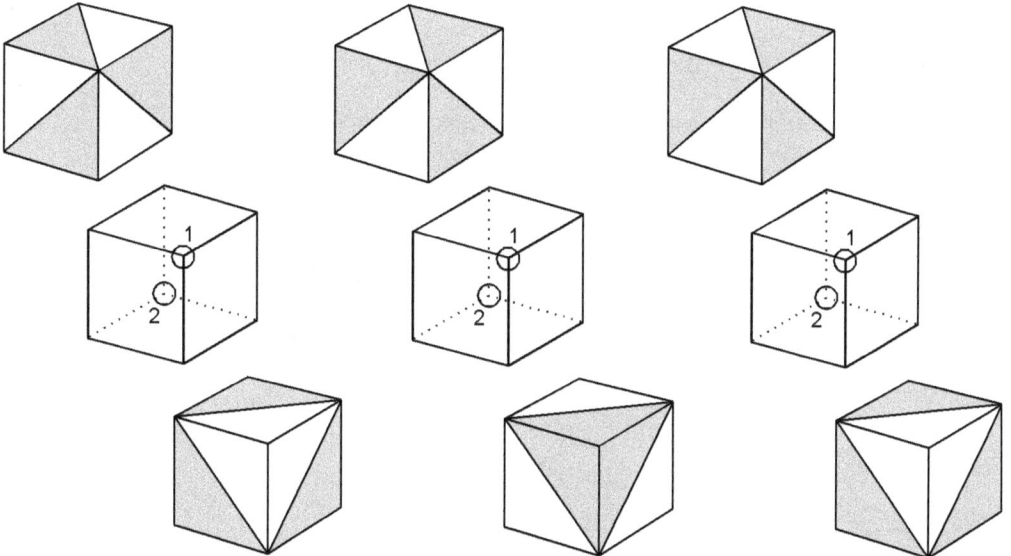

20. The same modules can be rearranged to make several other cubes including the three shown here. All these cubes are irregular. It is not possible to produce a cube that carries the same pattern front and back using six identical Yin Yang modules.

Making mirror-image modules
Begin by folding a module in the normal way to step 14.

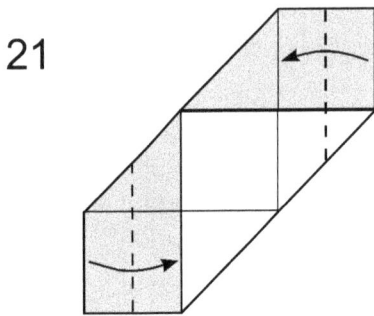

21

21. Fold the left and right hand edges inwards.

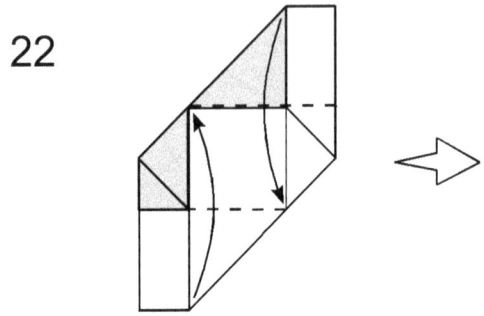

22

22. Fold the top and bottom edges inwards using the existing creases.

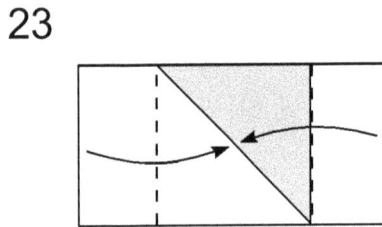

23

23. Fold the left and right edges to the centre using the existing creases.

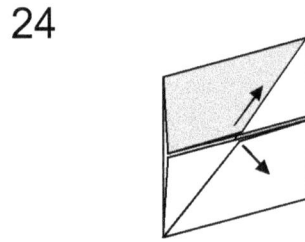

24

24. Rotate to look like this then open out both tabs at right angles.

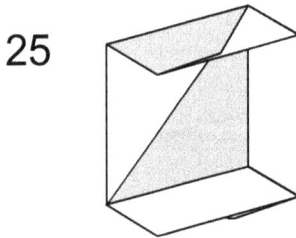

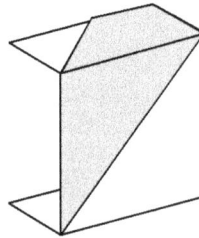

25

26. The mirror-image module is finished. You will need three of these.

David Mitchell / Building with Butterflies

26

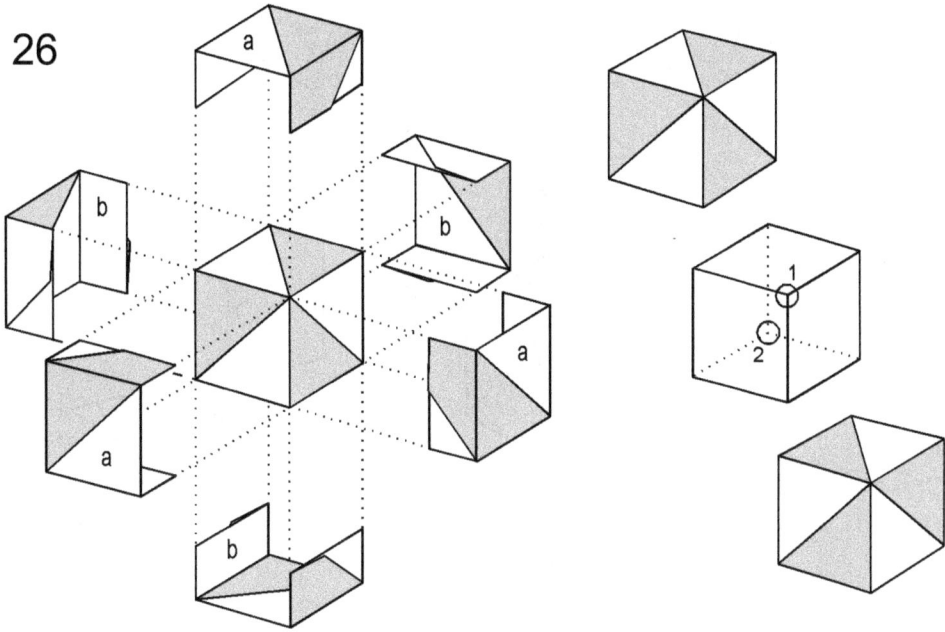

26. Three modules of each type, marked a and b in this picture, can be assembled to form the cube shown here, where the pattern on the back is the negative of the pattern on the front.

27

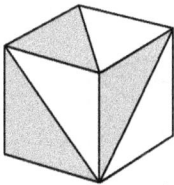
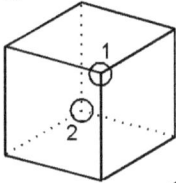
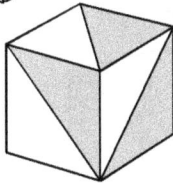

28

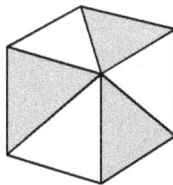
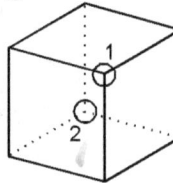
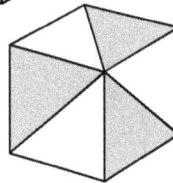
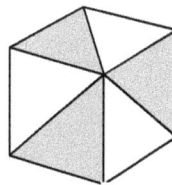
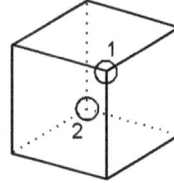
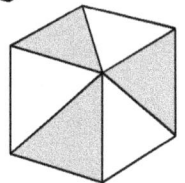

27. This is the same cube viewed from a different direction.

28. The modules can be rearranged to make two cubes which are patterned the same front and back.

29

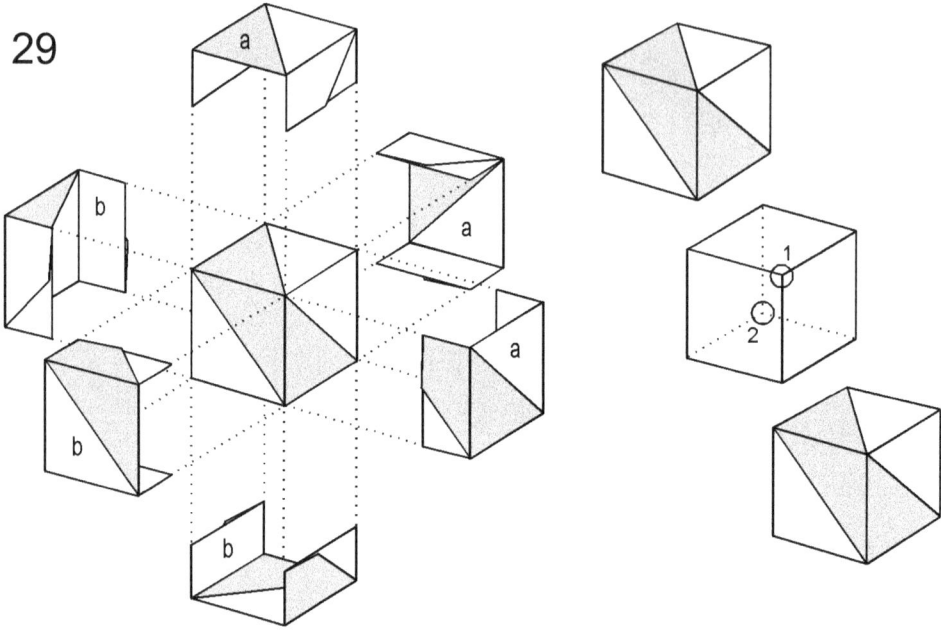

29. The modules can also be arranged to produce a cube with a single coloured stripe around the faces.

30

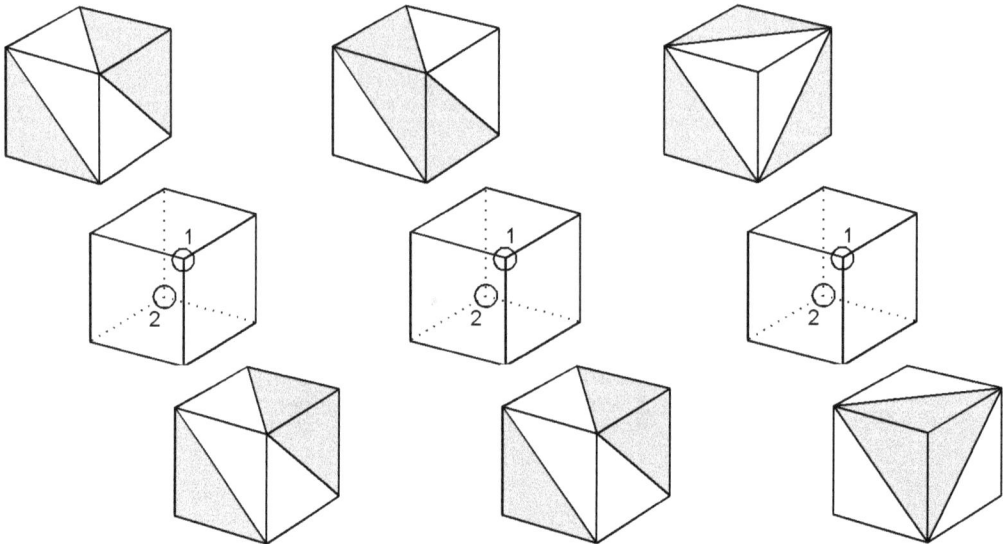

30. These three cubes are also possible. This does not exhaust the possibilities.

David Mitchell / Building with Butterflies

Single Diagonal Stripe Cubes

The design of these cubes makes use of mirror-image and negative modules to unusual effect. The Op-Art Effect Cube is particularly striking.

Begin by following steps 1 to 8 of the Chequerboard Cube (see page 21).

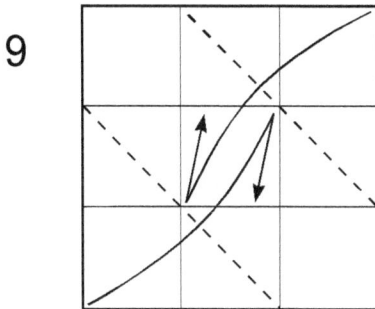

9. Fold two opposite corners diagonally inwards as shown, then unfold.

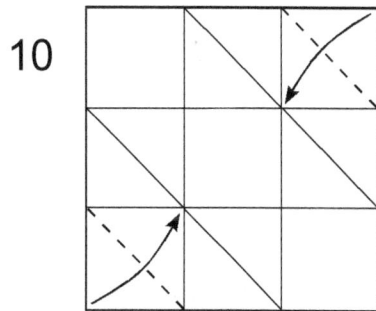

10. Fold the same corners inwards again.

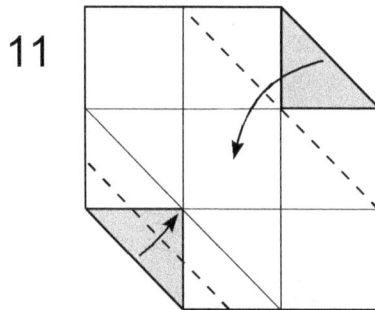

11. And again. Note that these two folds are not symmetrical.

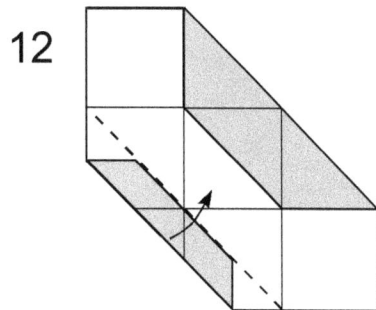

12. Fold the bottom left hand corner inwards using the crease made in step 9.

13

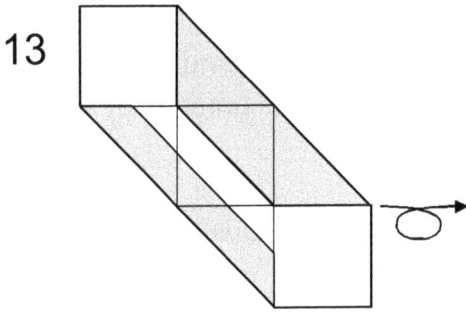

13. Turn over sideways.

14

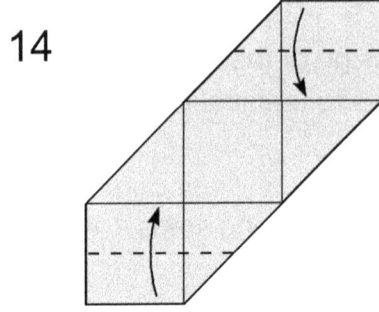

14. Fold the top and bottom edges inwards.

15

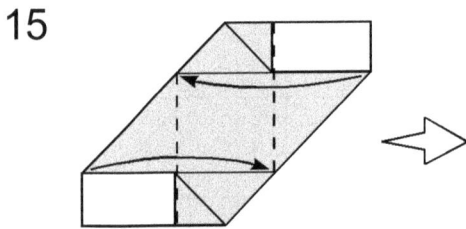

15. Fold the left and right edges inwards as well using the existing creases,

16

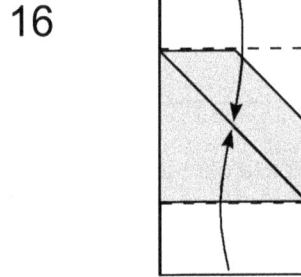

16. Fold the top and bottom edges into the centre using the existing creases.

17

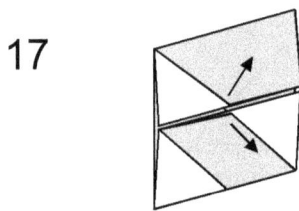

17. Open out both tabs at right angles.

18

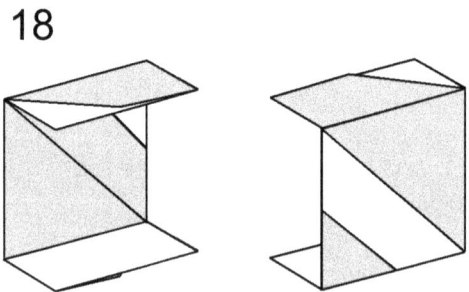

18. Make three modules like this.

David Mitchell / Building with Butterflies

Making mirror-image modules
Begin by folding your remaining three squares to step 14.

19

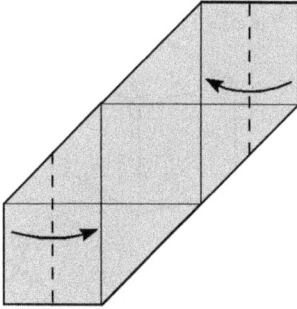

19. Fold the left and right edges inwards.

20

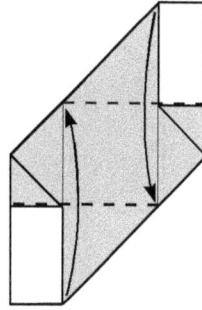

20. Fold the top and bottom edges inwards using the existing creases.

21

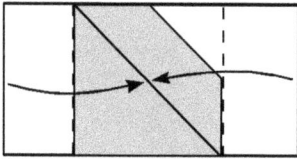

21. Fold the left and right edges into the centre using the existing creases.

22

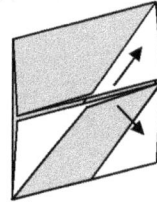

22. Rotate the design to look like this then open both tabs at right angles.

23

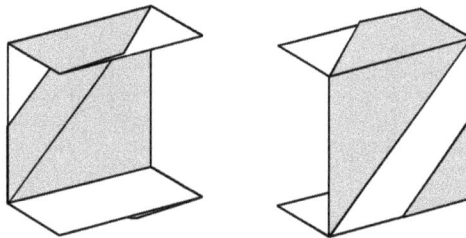

23. Make three of these as well.

24

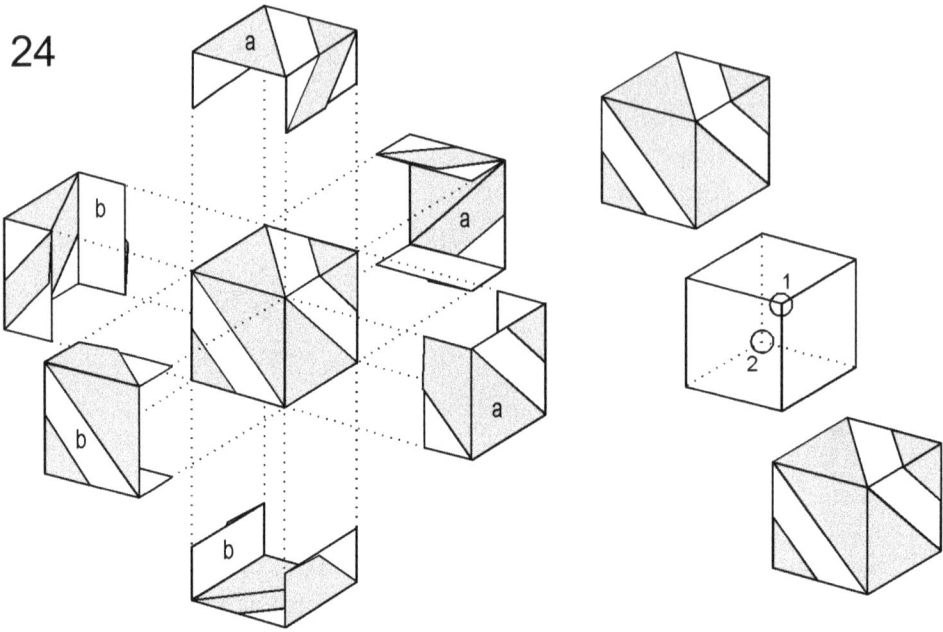

24. Both white stripes run all the way around the cube.

25

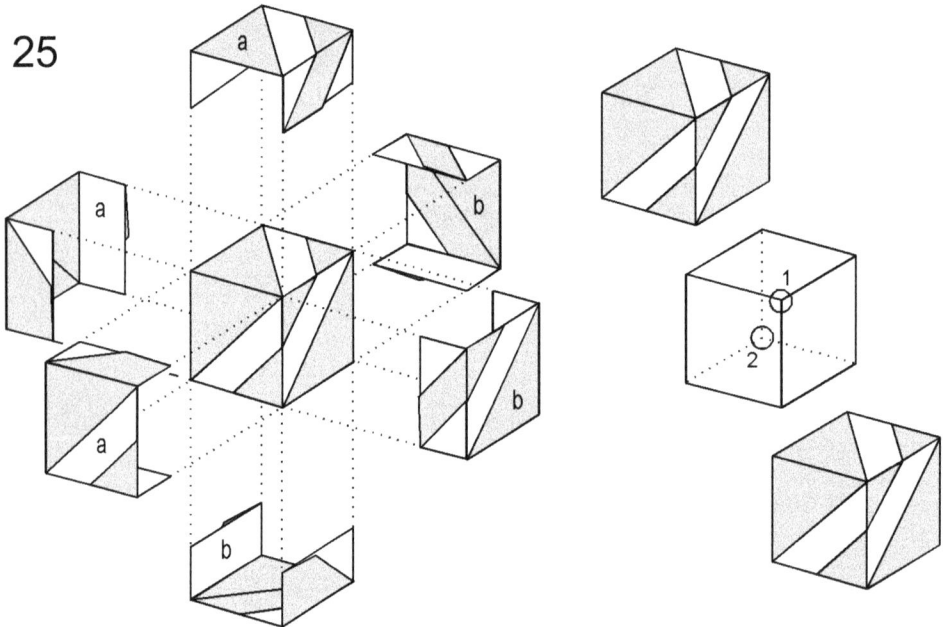

25. This is the Op Art Effect Cube.

David Mitchell / Building with Butterflies

Making negative modules
You can produce negative modules by arranging your paper the other way up before you start to fold.

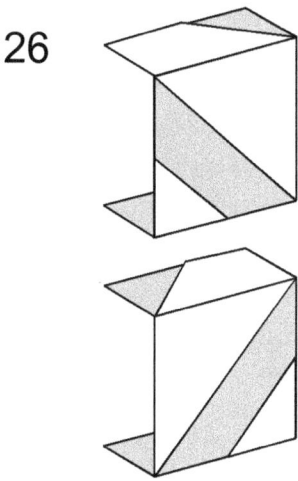

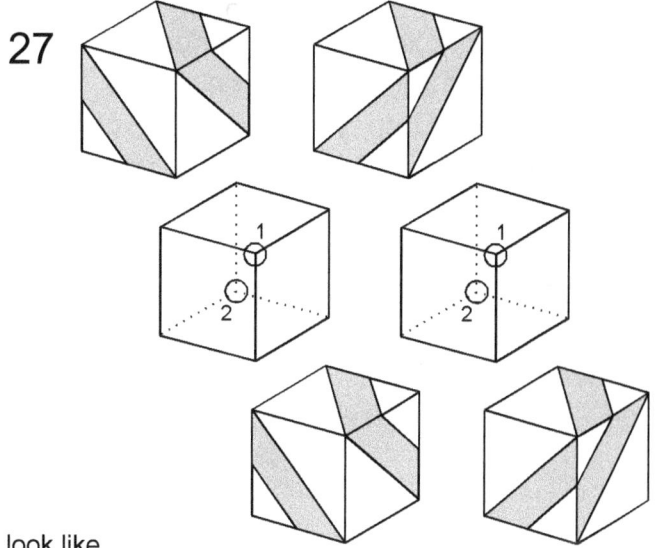

26

27

26. The negative modules will look like this.

27. And the negative cubes like this.

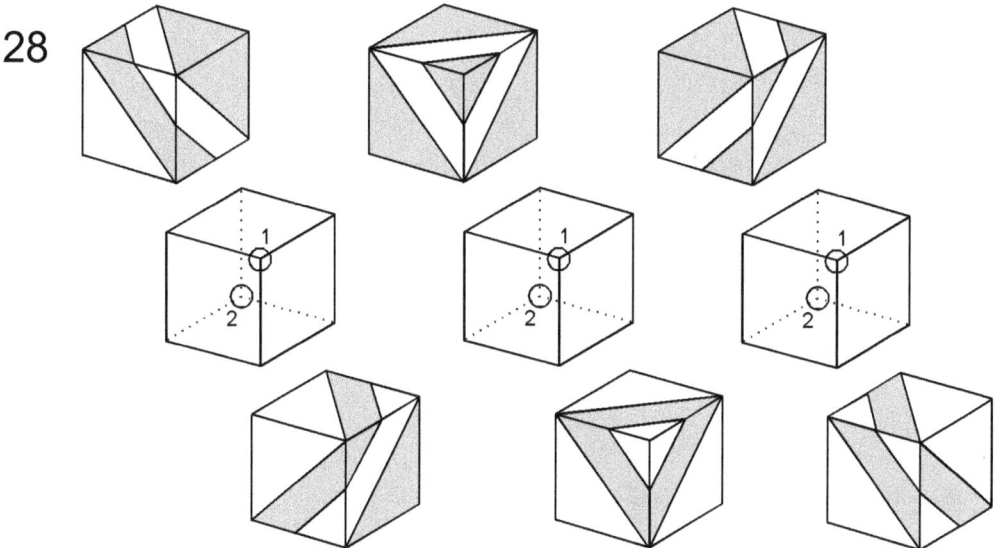

28

28. You can also create cubes by combining positive and negative modules.

Double Diagonal Stripe Cubes

These strikingly patterned cubes are built from compound modules, each of which is made from two squares of irogami, so that you will need twelve square sheets of paper in all to make a cube.

Begin by folding the standard modules for Paul Jackson's Cube from six of these squares (see pages 12 and 13). The remaining squares are folded into piggyback modules by following the instructions below. Half these modules are folded as mirror-images of the other half.

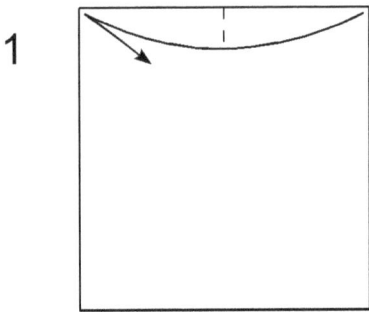

1

1. Make a tiny crease to mark the centre of the top edge.

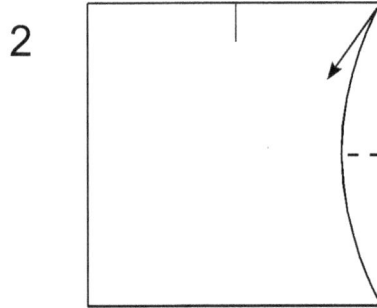

2

2. Make a tiny crease to mark the centre of the right hand edge.

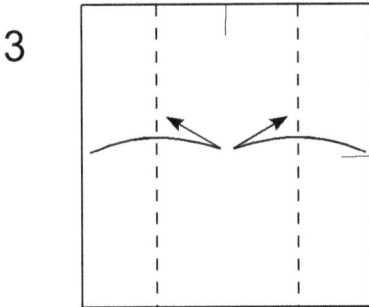

3

3. Fold the left and right hand edges into the centre, then unfold.

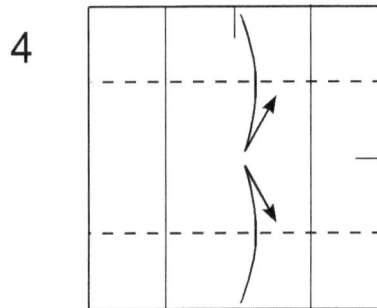

4

4. Fold the top and bottom edges into the centre, then unfold.

David Mitchell / Building with Butterflies

5

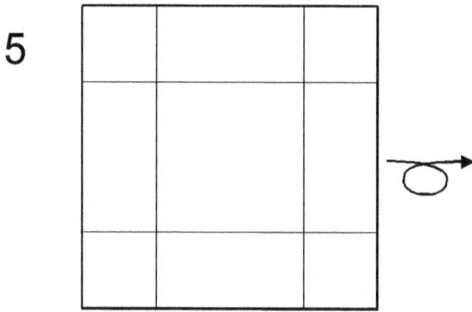

5. Turn over sideways.

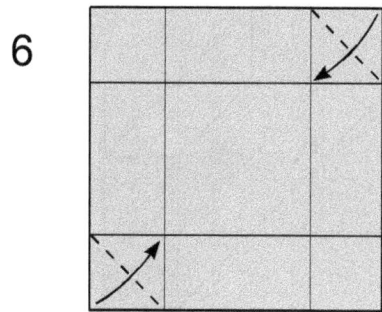

6

6. Fold the top right and bottom left corners inwards.

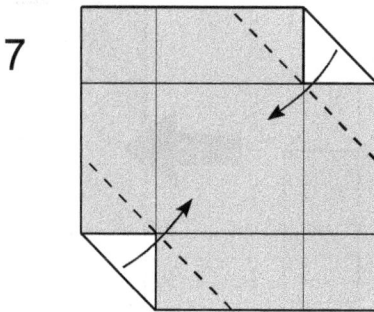

7

7. Fold the same corners inwards again making sure that the creases line up in the way shown in picture 8.

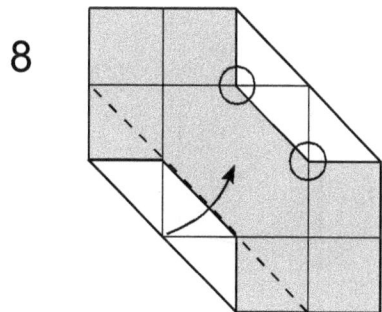

8

8. Fold the bottom left hand corner inwards for a third time. Make sure the corners end up in the positions marked with circles in picture 9.

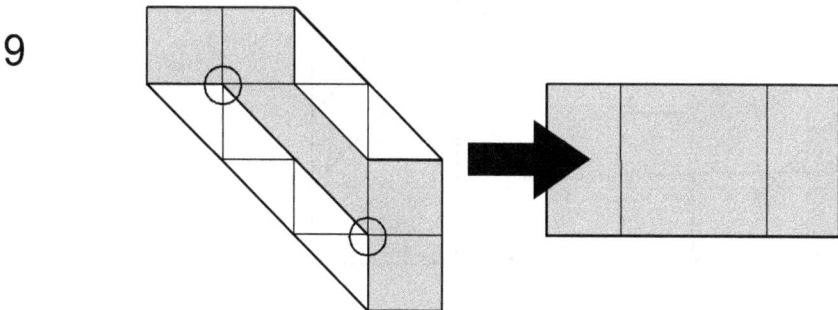

9

9. Lay the piggyback module on top of a standard module. Picture 10 shows you how they should be aligned.

10

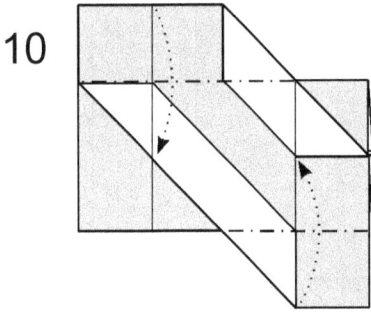

10. Wrap the top and bottom edges of the piggyback module backwards around the standard module using the existing creases.

11

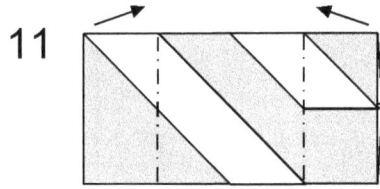

11. Fold the left and right ends of the compound module backwards at right angles. Take care not to distort the module as you do this.

12

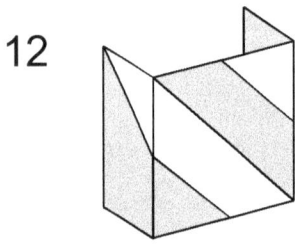

13

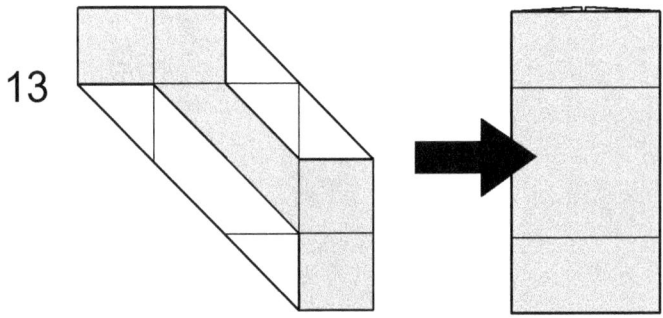

12. Make three modules like this. To make the three mirror-image modules follow steps 1 through 8 then 13 to 16.

13. Lay a piggyback module on top of a standard module like this. Picture 14 shows you how they should be aligned.

14

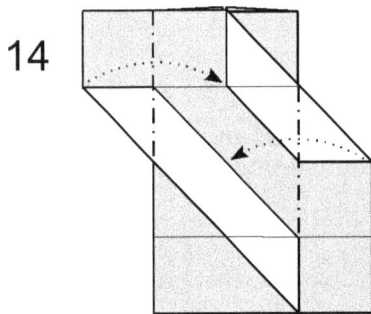

15

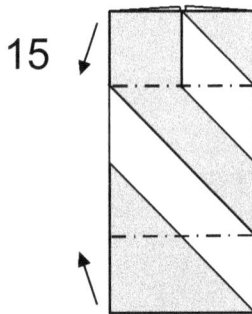

16

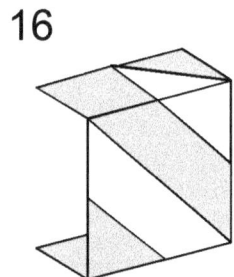

14. Wrap the right and left edges of the piggyback module backwards around the standard module using the existing creases.

15. Fold the top and bottom ends backwards at right angles. Take care not to distort the module as you do this.

16. Make three modules like this as well.

David Mitchell / Building with Butterflies

17

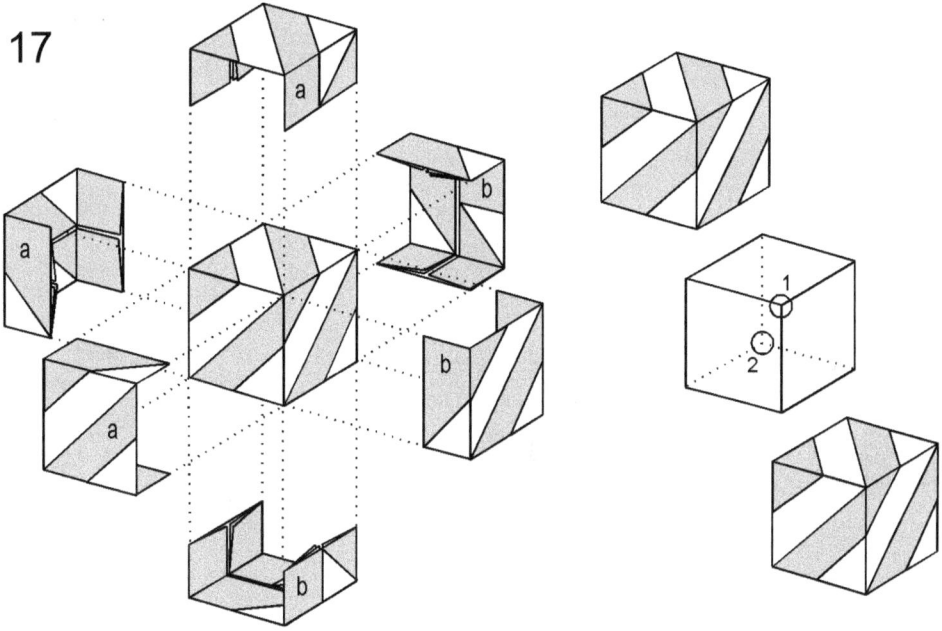

17. The stripes run all the way round the cube.

18

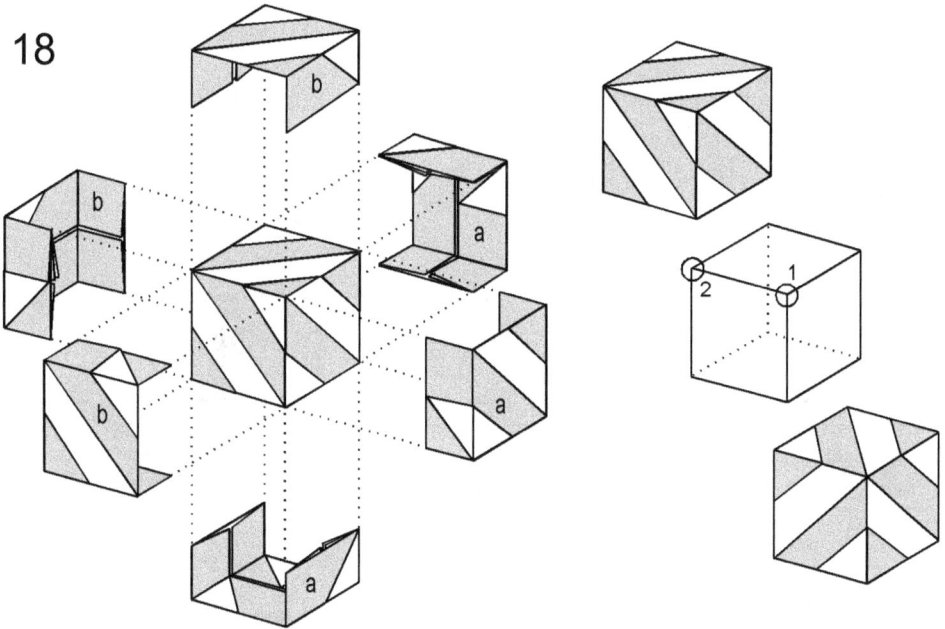

18. This cube only appears to be patterned in a regular way when viewed along one particular axis of symmetry.

19

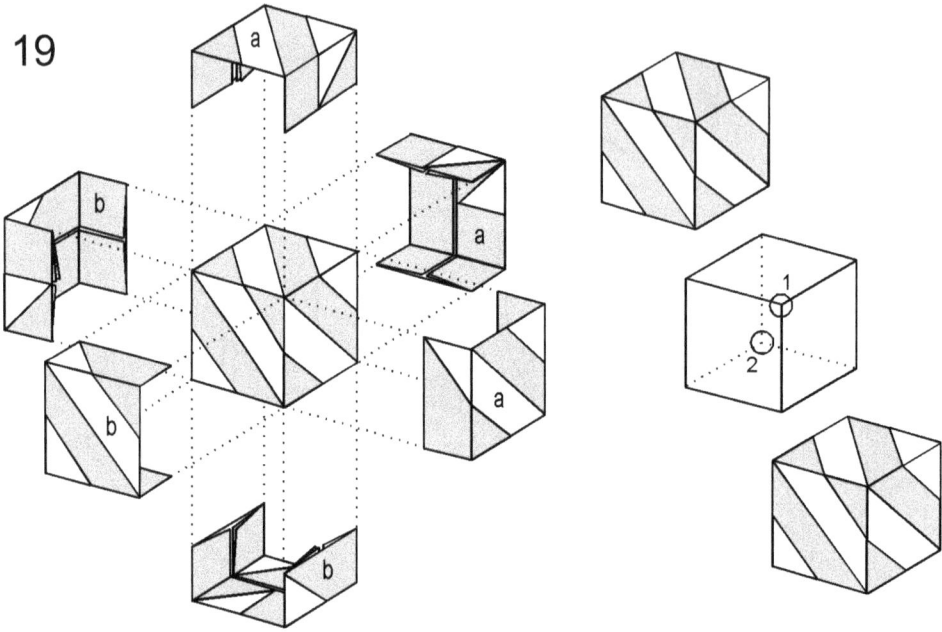

19. The same modules will go together to form a more complex Op Art Effect Cube.

20

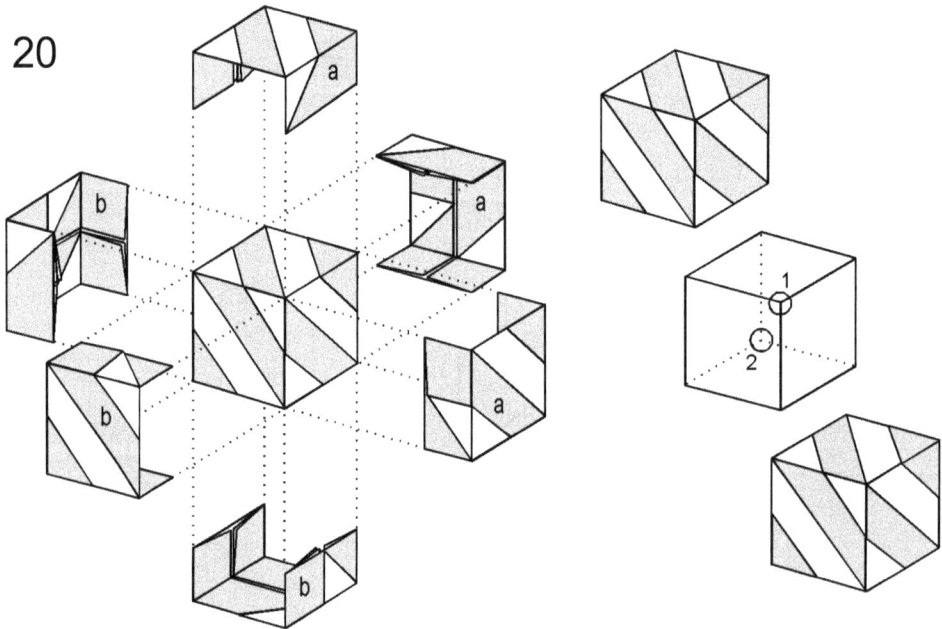

20. They can also be assembled into a negative version.

David Mitchell / Building with Butterflies

A Homage to Paul Jackson's Cube

Distortions

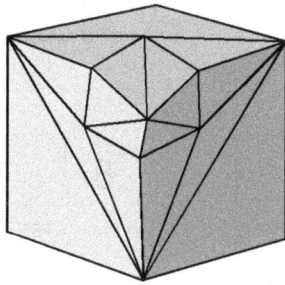

The Columbus Cube

The Columbus Cube is created by turning one corner of Paul Jackson's Cube inside out. You will need six squares of paper. Three of the modules are standard modules. The other three modules are folded by following steps 1 to 4 on page 12 and then steps 5 to 9 below.

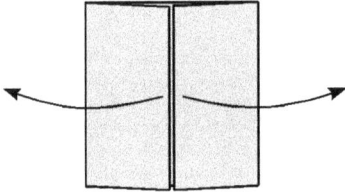

5. Arrange like this then undo the folds made in step 4.

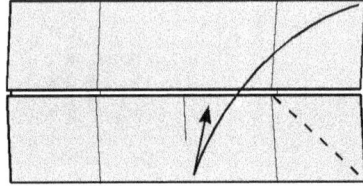

6. Fold the right hand edge onto the bottom edge, crease half way across the diagonal, then unfold.

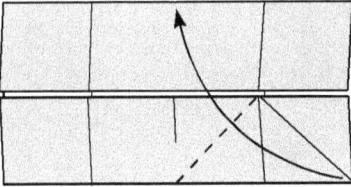

7. Fold the right hand edge onto the top edge but only crease half way across the diagonal.

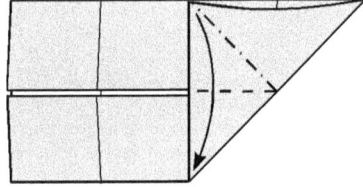

8. Fold the left hand edge of the front layer in half downwards and flatten the layers into the position shown in picture 9.

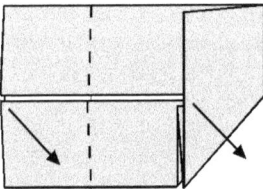

9. Open both flaps up at right angles and stand upright on the flat end.

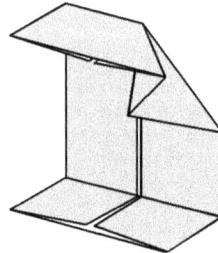

10. Your module will look like this. Make three.

11

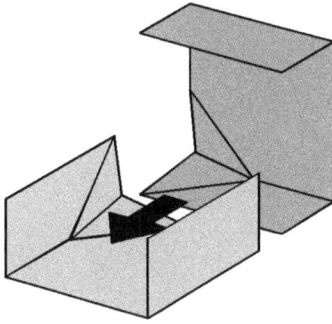

11. Slide two modules together like this

12

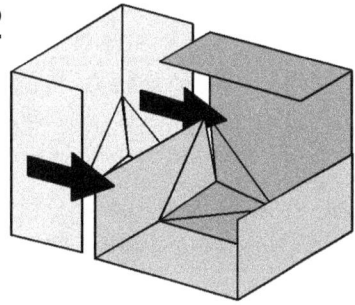

12. Add a third to complete the inverted corner.

13

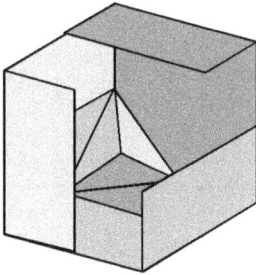

13. At this stage the modules should already hold together quite firmly.

14

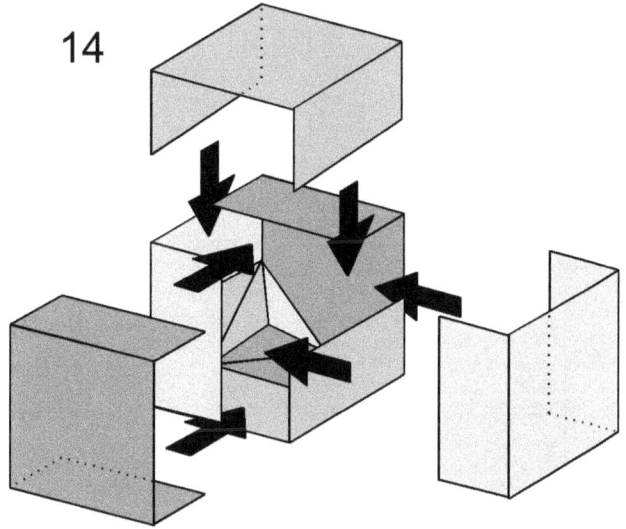

14. Add the three standard modules like this.

15

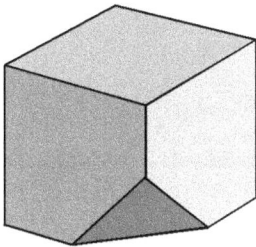

15. The Columbus Cube is finished.

16

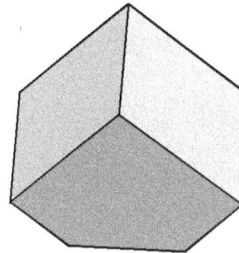

16. The Columbus Cube can be stood, point upwards, on the inverted corner.

The Tetracube

The Tetracube is made by turning four of the six corners of Paul Jackson's Cube inside out (specifically those corners that lie at the vertices of a tetrahedron inscribed within the cube).

You will need six squares of paper. Begin by following steps 1 to 4 on page 12 then follow steps 5 to 9 below.

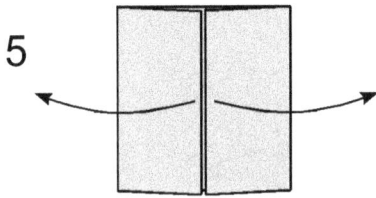

5. Arrange like this then undo the folds made in step 4.

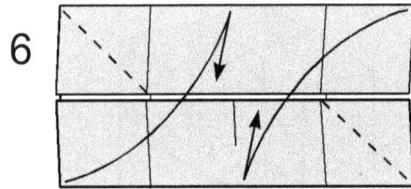

6. Fold the right hand edge onto the bottom edge, crease half way across the diagonal, then unfold. Then fold the left hand edge onto the top edge, crease half way across the diagonal, and unfold.

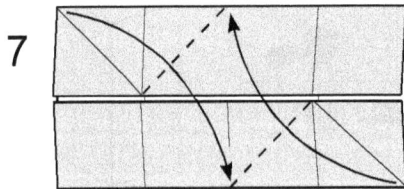

7. Fold the top left and bottom right corners inwards as shown but only crease halfway across the diagonals.

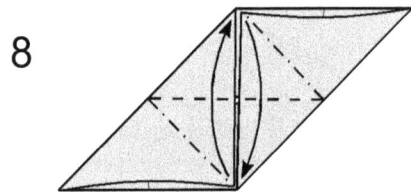

8. Fold the central edges of both front flaps in half and flatten the layers into the position shown in picture 9.

9

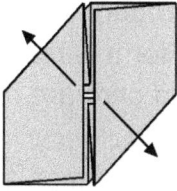

9. Open both front flaps at right angles to create the tabs then stand the module upright.

10

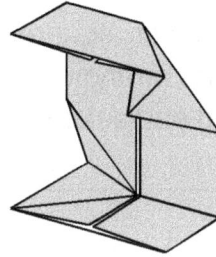

10. Make six.

11

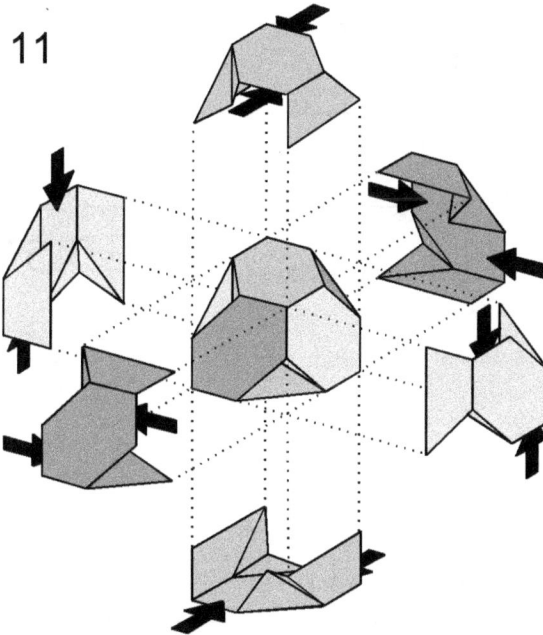

11. The modules go together like this. This looks complicated but is actually quite easy.

12

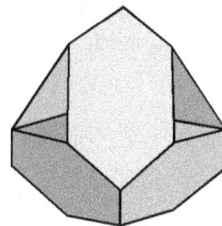

12. The Tetracube is finished.

The Paul Jackson Cuboctahedron

Inverting all six corners of Paul Jackson's Cube produces a cuboctahedron with sunken triangular faces. This form is robust but correspondingly difficult to assemble. Patience and care are required.

You will need six squares of paper. Begin by following steps 1 to 3 on page 12 and arranging your paper in the way shown in picture 4 below. You should particularly note the position of the small central crease.

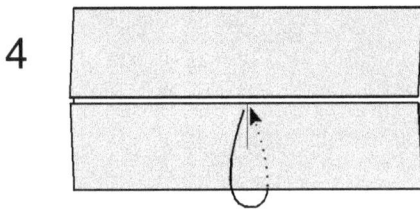

4. Rotate the bottom front flap out of sight behind by reversing the direction of the existing crease.

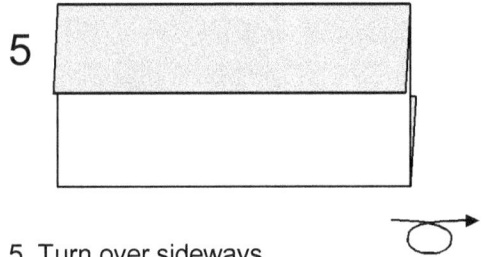

5. Turn over sideways.

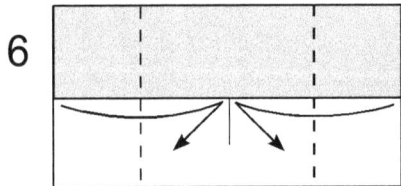

6. Fold both outside edges to the centre using the small central crease as a guide, then unfold.

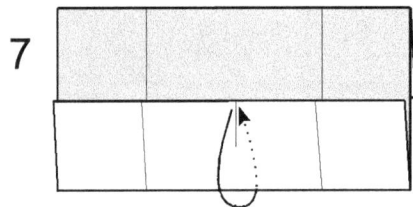

7. Rotate the front flap out of sight behind by reversing the direction of the existing crease.

8

8. Turn over sideways.

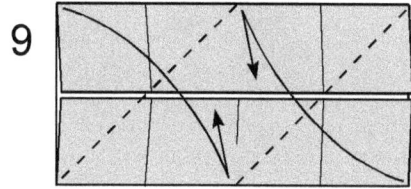

9

9. Fold the right hand edge onto the top edge and the left hand edge onto the bottom edge, then unfold.

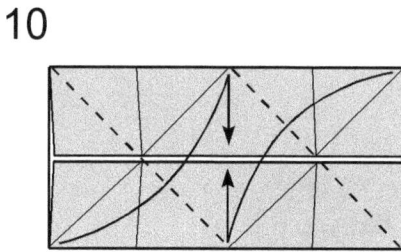

10

10. Fold the right hand edge onto the bottom edge and the left hand edge onto the top edge, then unfold.

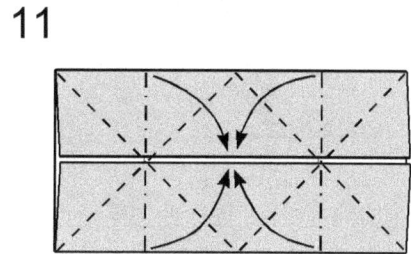

11

11. Collapse the module into the form shown in picture 12.

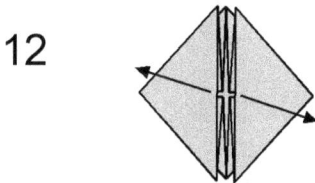

12

12. Open out both front flaps at right angles.

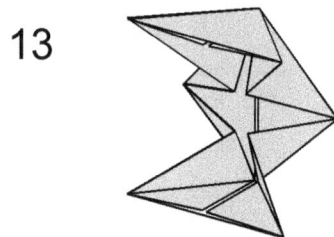

13

13. This is what the finished module should look like.

14

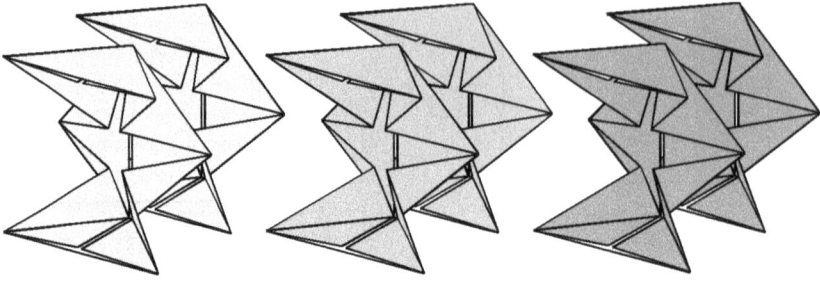

14. Make six.

15

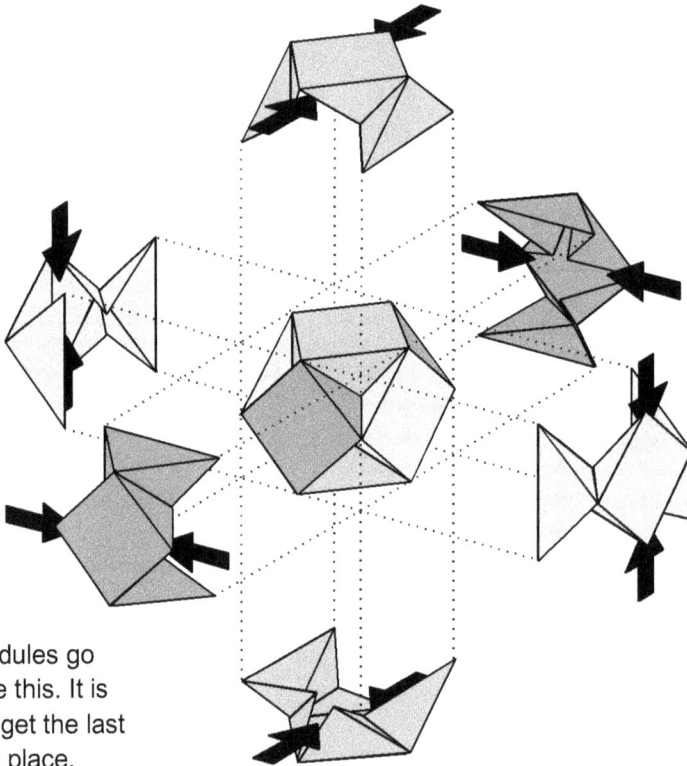

15. The modules go together like this. It is not easy to get the last module into place.

16

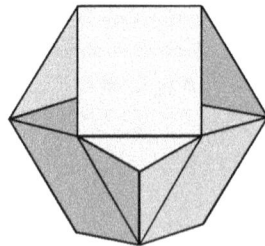

16. The Paul Jackson Cuboctahedron is finished.

David Mitchell / Building with Butterflies

Metamorphosis

The Metamorphosis transformation is an attractive way of inverting the corner of a cube that produces a hexagonal indentation surrounded by a triangular bulge. I have used this transformation in many designs but still feel it is seen to its best advantage here.

You will need six square sheets of paper. Three of the modules are standard modules (see page 13). The other three are folded by following steps 1 to 4 on page 12 then steps 5 to 20 below.

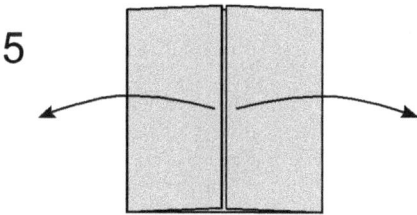

5

5. Arrange like this then undo the folds made in step 4.

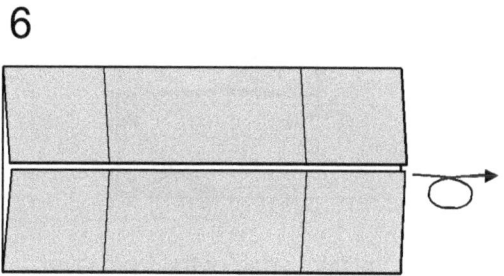

6

6. Turn over sideways.

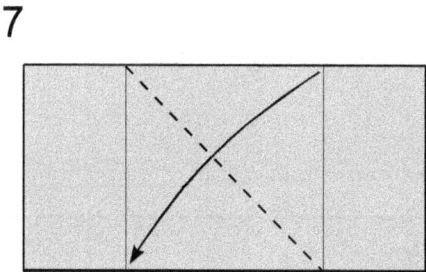

7

7. Make a diagonal fold across the central square by folding the point where the right hand crease intersects the top edge onto the point where the left hand crease intersects the bottom edge.

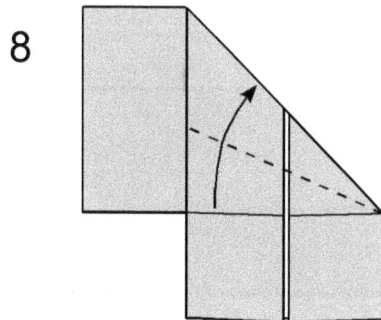

8

8. Fold the horizontal crease onto the sloping edge.

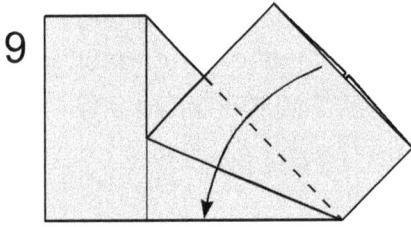

9. Fold the sloping top edge of the front flap inwards and downwards using the existing crease.

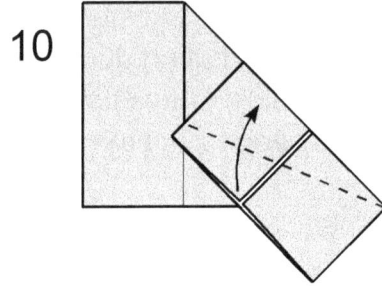

10. Fold the bottom edge of the front layer upwards so that the new folded edge lines up with the existing folded edge behind it.

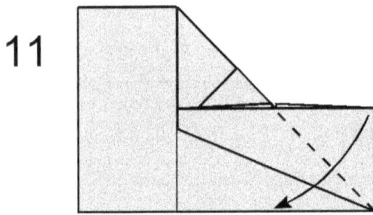

11. Fold the right edge of the front layer onto the bottom edge.

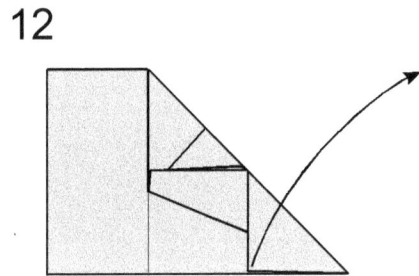

12. Open out folds 7 through 11.

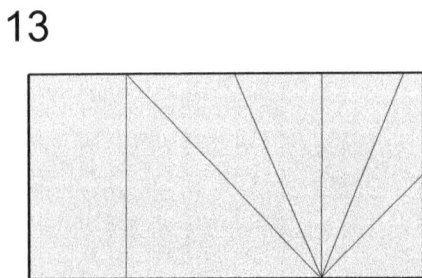

13. Make sure you have made all the creases shown here. Turn over sideways.

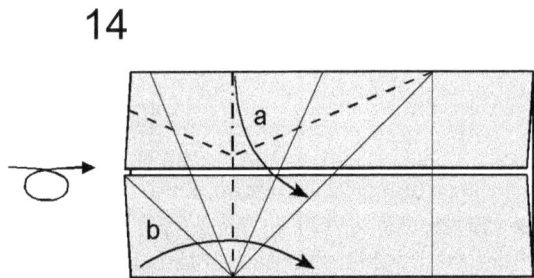

14. Make fold a, then fold b, flatten the layers and crease firmly.

15

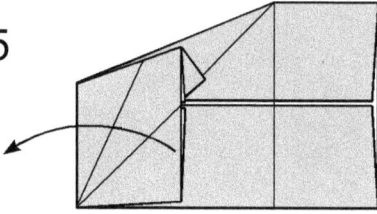

15. Open out fold 14.

16

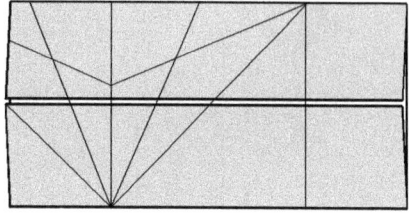

16. Turn over sideways.

17

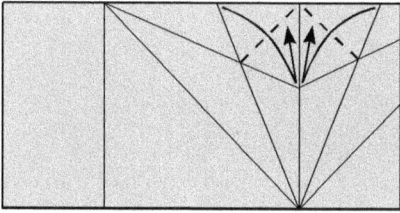

17. Make two more small creases in the way shown here.

18

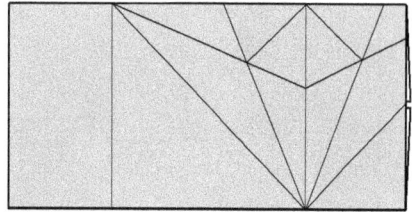

18. Check that you have made all the creases shown here.

19

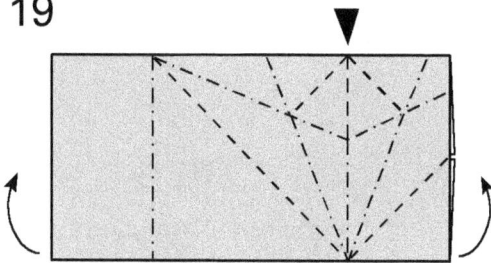

19. Collapse the module into the shape shown in picture 20.

20

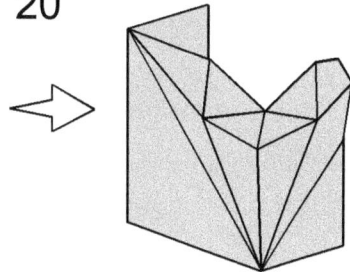

20. Make three.

21

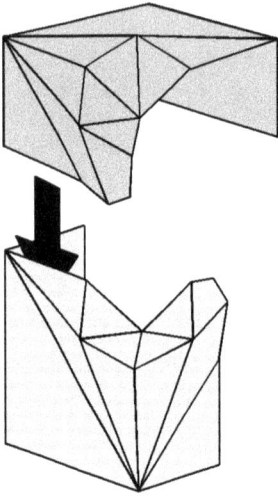

21. The first two modules go together like this.

22

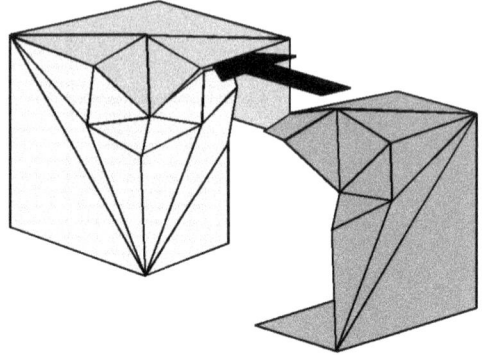

22. Add the third module to complete the front corner.

23

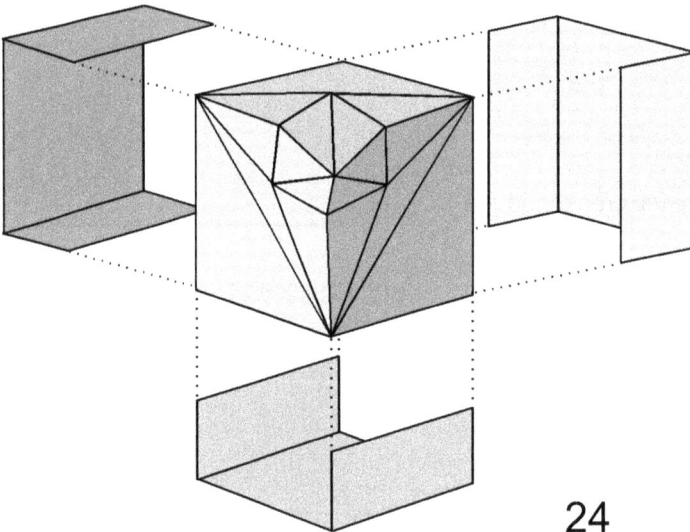

23. Add the three standard modules to complete the back corner as well.

24

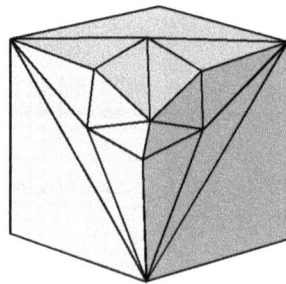

24. Metamorphosis is finished.

David Mitchell / Building with Butterflies

Metamorphosis 2

This second Metamorphosis transformation is similar to the first except that the indentation is triangular rather than hexagonal.

You will need six square sheets of paper. Three of the modules are standard modules (see page 13). The other three are folded by following steps 1 to 4 on page 12, steps 5 to 18 on pages 49 to 51 then 19 to 30 below.

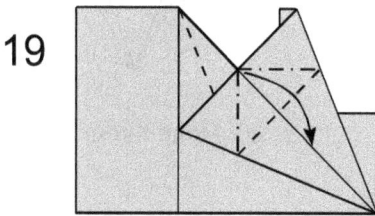

19. Collapse the paper into the form shown in picture 20.

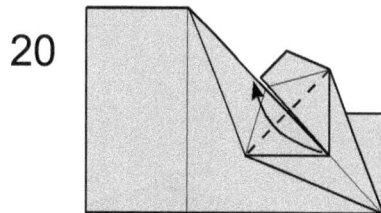

20. Make a new crease across the front layer to join the ends of the existing short horizontal and vertical creases. The paper will collapse into the form shown in picture 21.

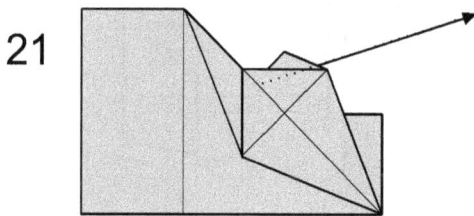

21. Fold the front flap upwards to the left as shown.

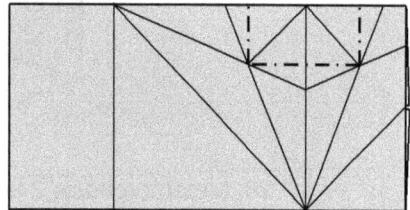

22. Open out the last three folds.

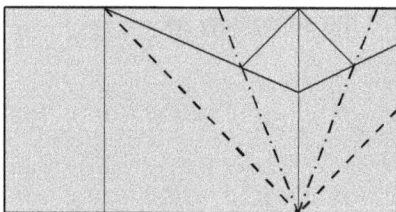

23. Reverse the direction of these three creases.

24

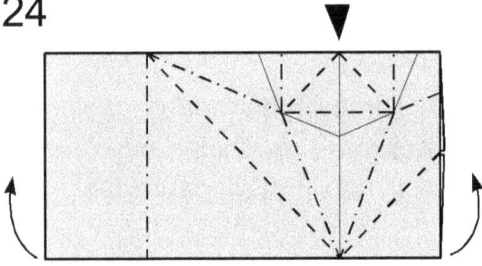

24. Collapse the module into the form shown in picture 25.

25

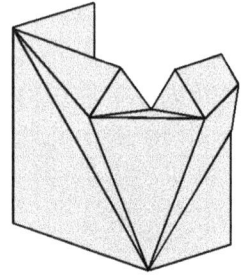

25. Make three.

26

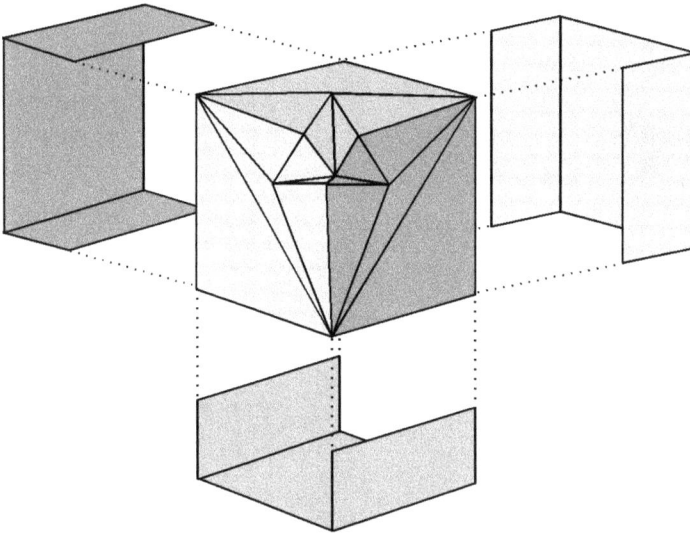

26. Metamorphosis 2 is assembled in the same way as Metamorphosis (see page 52).

The Icarus Cube

The Icarus Cube is created by bringing out the centre of the faces of the cube to form wings (which also act as springs to produce tension within the structure). You can do this from a square but the module then only has a single thickness of paper along the open edges, which weakens the final form. Folding from a 2x1 rectangle solves this problem.

You will need three large squares to create the 2x1 rectangles from. If you are using irogami begin with your paper arranged white side up.

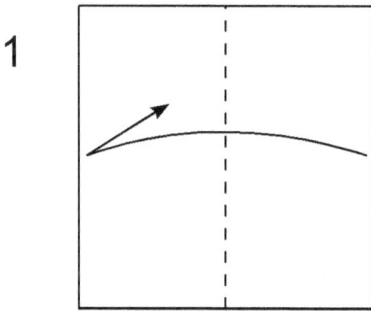

1. Fold in half sideways, then unfold.

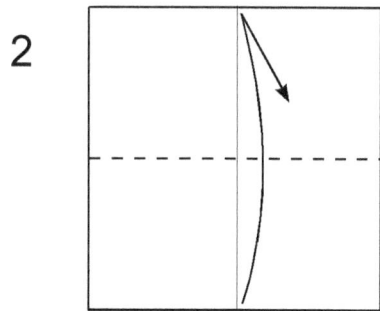

2. Fold in half upwards, then unfold.

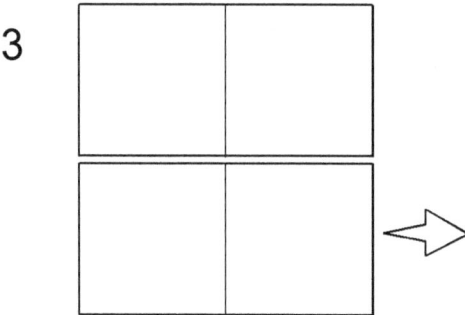

3. Cut in half along the horizontal crease.

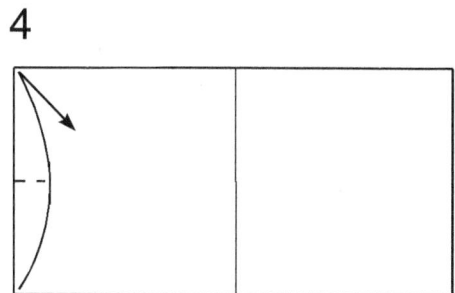

4. Make a tiny crease to mark the centre of the left hand edge.

5

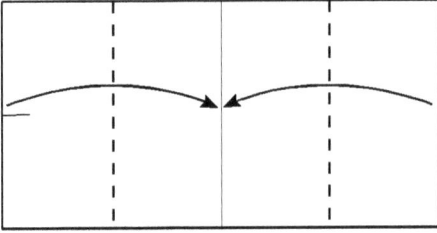

5. Fold both outside edges into the centre.

6

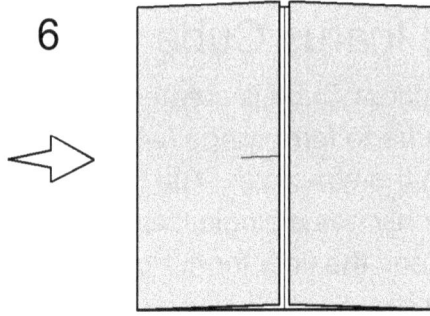

6. You could, if you wish, start from this point using a square of thick paper, but the result is not so good.

7

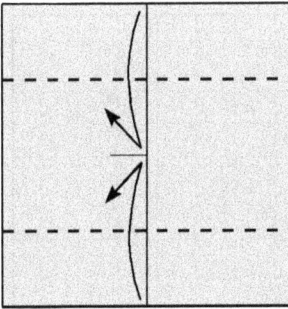

7. Fold the top and bottom edges into the centre, then unfold.

8

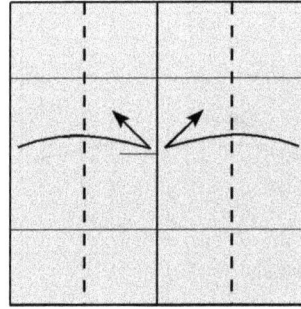

8. Fold both outside edges into the centre, then unfold.

9

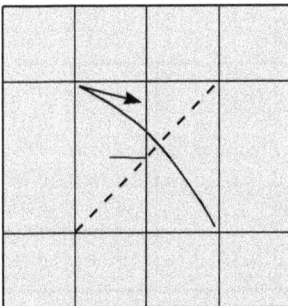

9. Fold in half diagonally, then unfold, but only crease across the centre section of the paper.

10

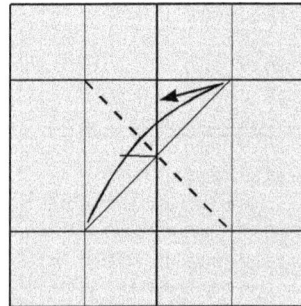

10. Fold in half diagonally in the opposite direction, then unfold, but only crease across the centre section of the paper.

11

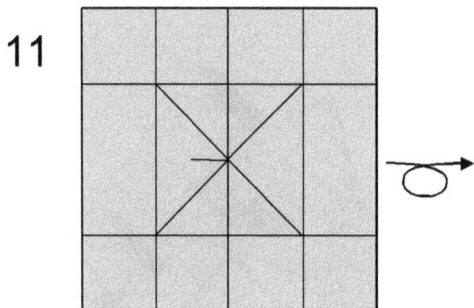

11. Turn over sideways.

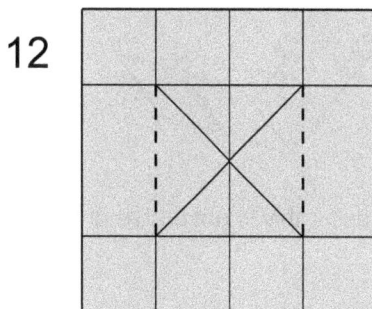

12

12. Reverse the direction of these two sections of crease.

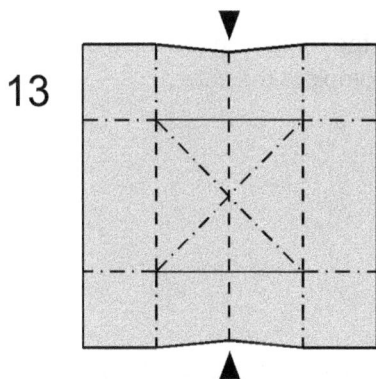

13

13. Collapse so that the centre of the paper rises up towards you.

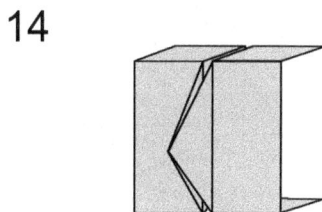

14

14. This is the Icarus module. Make six.

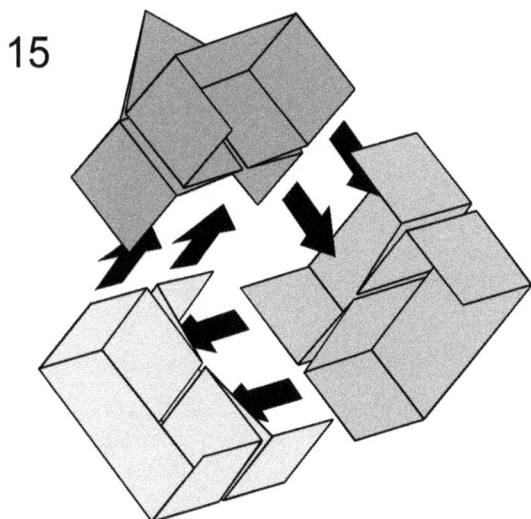

15

15. Three modules go together like this to form the back corner of the cube.

16

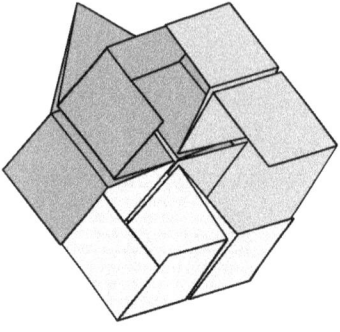

16. The assembly is not stable at this point.

17

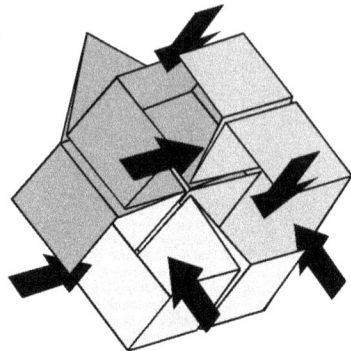

17. Add the remaining modules one by one to complete the cube.

18

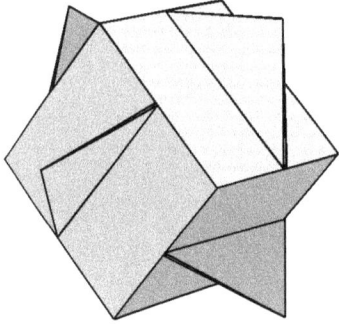

18. Squeeze the modules together so that the assembly becomes robust. The Icarus Cube is finished

A Homage to Paul Jackson's Cube

The Sculptures

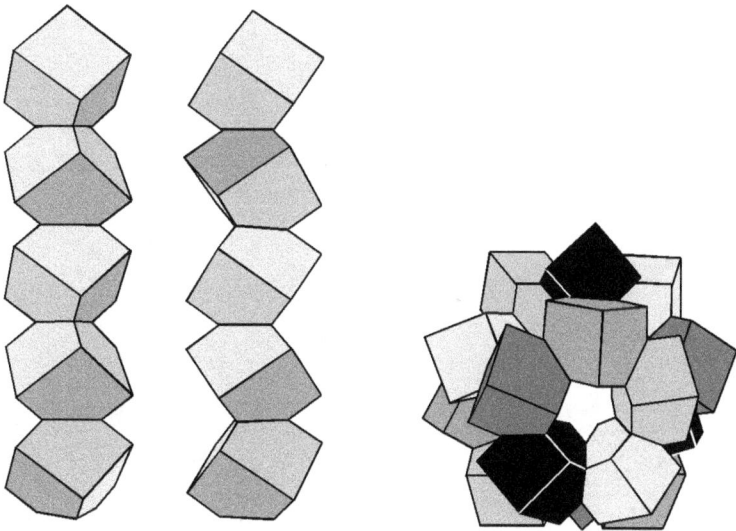

The Columbus Tower

The Columbus Tower is built by the simple expedient of stacking Columbus Cubes on top of each other.

1

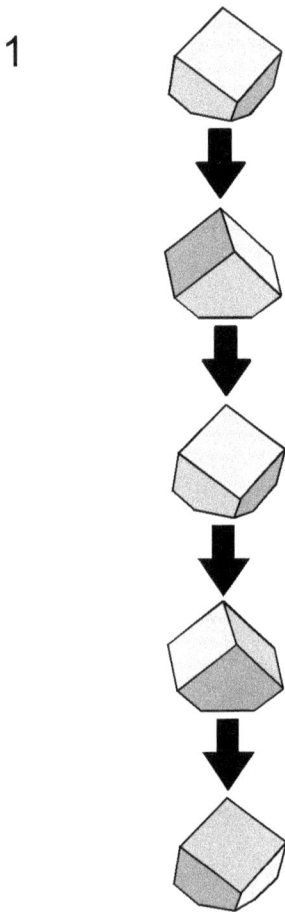

1. Five cubes is probably the optimum size of the stack.

2

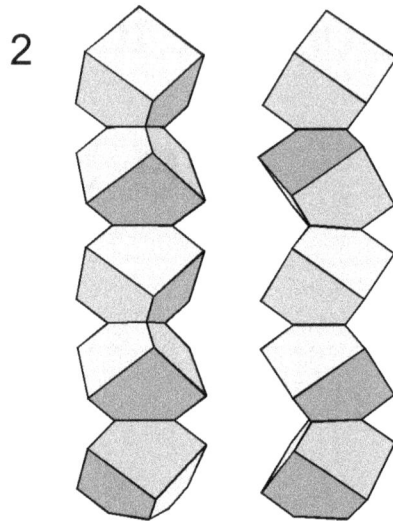

2. The Columbus Tower is a strangely beautiful sculpture.

3

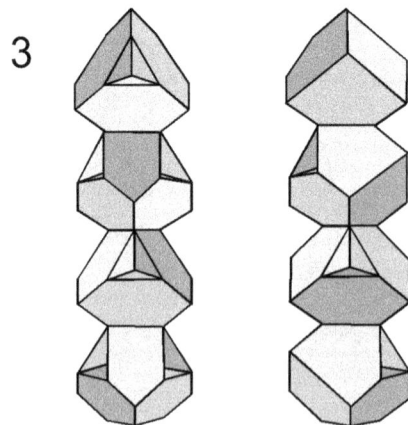

3. Tetracubes and other Columbus Cube variants can also be stacked in this way.

David Mitchell / Building with Butterflies

The Columbus Pyramid

The Columbus Pyramid is made by first combining Columbus Cubes into layers, or tiers, by the use of joining pieces, then stacking them to form a pyramid. On their own the tiers would stack to form a smooth sided pyramid of little interest. The secret lies in the use of link units to separate the tiers. This not only breaks up the smooth sides of the pyramid but also introduces light into the structure and creates interior space.

The number of square sheets of paper required for the sculpture will vary depending on the number of tiers you intend to include.

Making the joining pieces

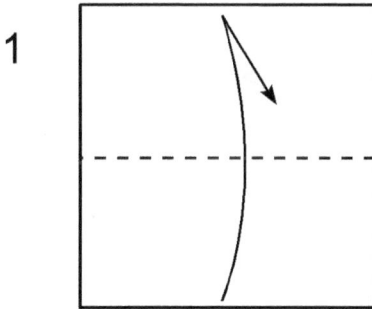

1. Begin with a square of paper the same size as the squares you are folding the Columbus Cubes from. Fold in half upwards, then unfold.

2. Cut along the horizontal crease.

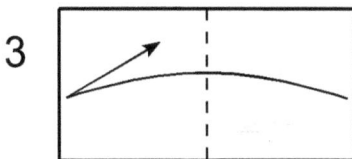

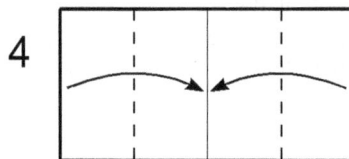

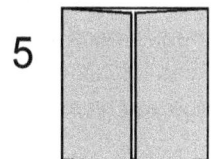

3. Fold in half sideways, then unfold.

4. Fold both outside edges to the centre.

5. The joining piece is finished.

Assembling Columbus Cubes into tiers

6

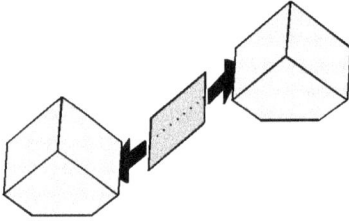

6. Join two Columbus Cubes together like this. The dotted line shows the position of the unfolded edges. Always use the joining pieces in this orientation.

7

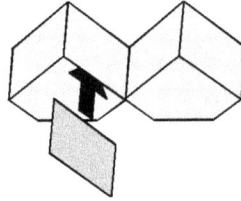

7. Add a second joining piece like this. Make sure you only slide joining pieces half way into the pockets.

8

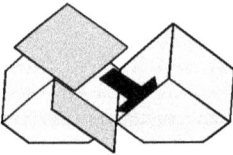

8. The third joining piece slides in like this.

9

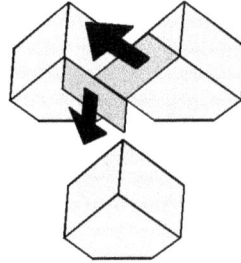

9. Add another cube to the front of the assembly. You may need to temporarily loosen the modules of this cube to achieve this.

10

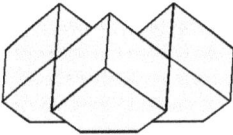

10. This is the result. Push all the modules back into place. The three cubes should hold together firmly once you have done this.

11

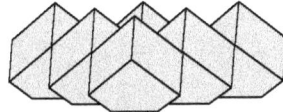

11. You can add further rows of Columbus Cubes to the assembly as required.

David Mitchell / Building with Butterflies

Making the link units

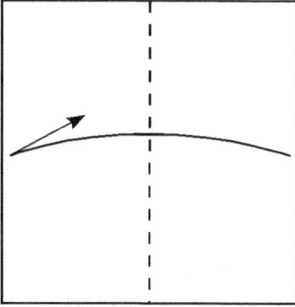

12. Begin with a square the same size as you are using to fold the Columbus Cubes from. Fold in half sideways, then unfold.

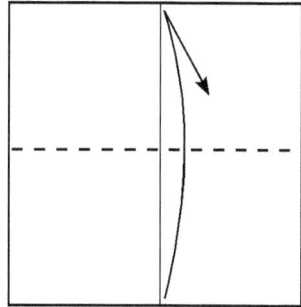

13. Fold in half upwards, then unfold.

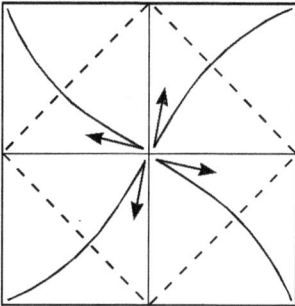

14. Fold all four corners into the centre, then unfold.

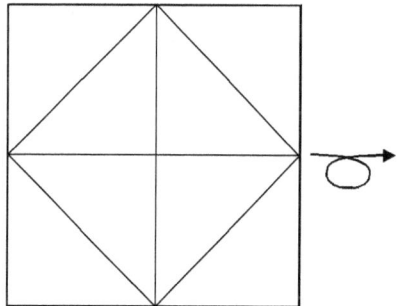

15. Turn over sideways.

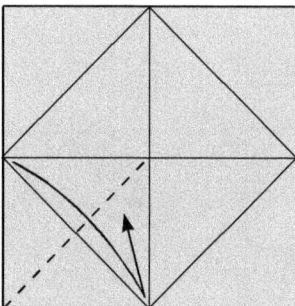

16. Make a crease across half of one diagonal.

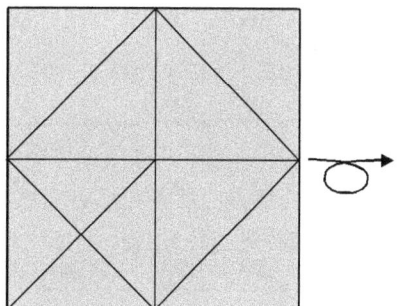

17. Turn over sideways again.

18

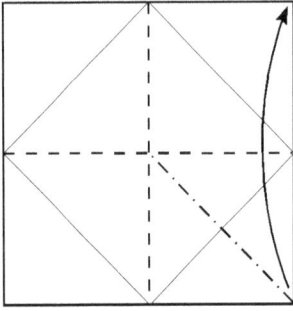

18. Fold the bottom right hand corner onto the top right corner. The paper becomes three dimensional as you do this.

19

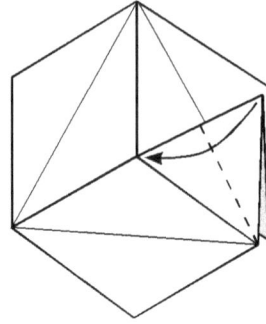

19. Fold the internal flap in half inwards using the existing crease.

20

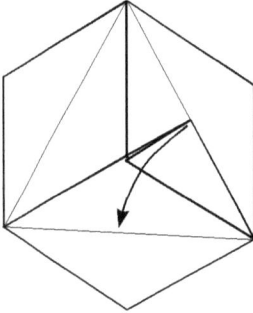

20. Fold the internal flap over to lock fold 19 in place.

21

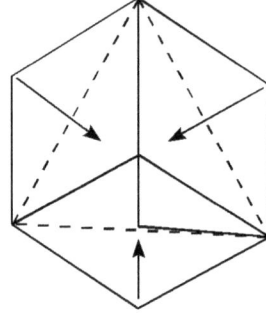

21. Fold all three corners inwards so that the edges almost meet (see picture 23).

22

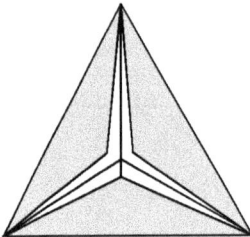

22. This is the result. From the side the unit now looks like picture 23.

23

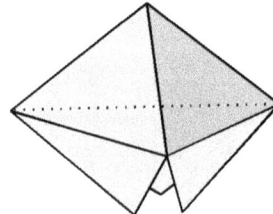

23. Note how the flaps at the bottom are arranged.

Building a five tier Columbus Pyramid

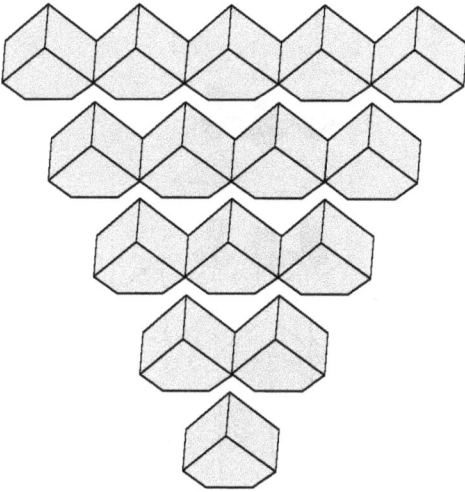

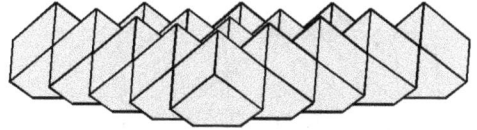

25. This is the result. Make sure all the modules that you loosened to assemble this tier have been pushed back together and that the structure of each of the cubes, and of the tier as a whole, is robust. This can take time and patience.

24. The base layer for a five tier Columbus Pyramid is built from fifteen Columbus Cubes. Join the cubes together using thirty joining pieces in the way shown in pictures 6 to 10.

26. Assemble a second tier from ten more Columbus Cubes.

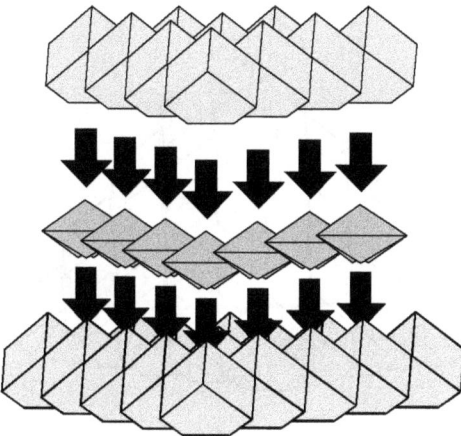

27. Drop ten link units into the holes in the top of the base tier then place the second tier of Columbus Cubes on top.

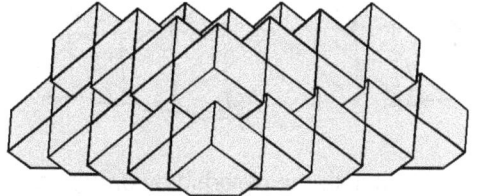

28. The result should look like this.

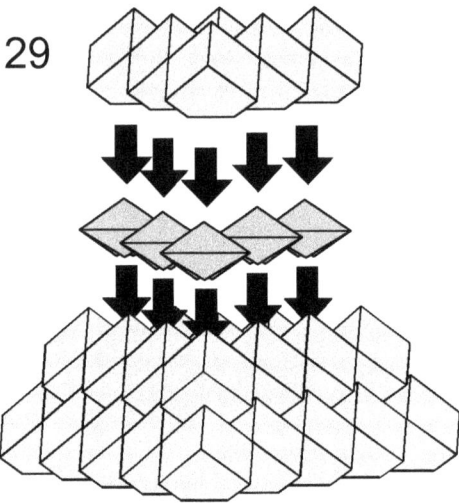

29. Assemble a third tier of six Columbus Cubes. Drop six link units into the holes in the top of the second tier and place the third tier on top.

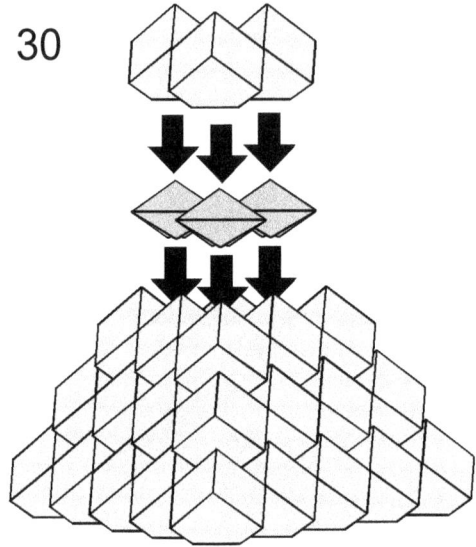

30. Assemble a fourth tier of just three Columbus Cubes. Drop three link units into the holes in the top of the third tier and place the fourth tier on top.

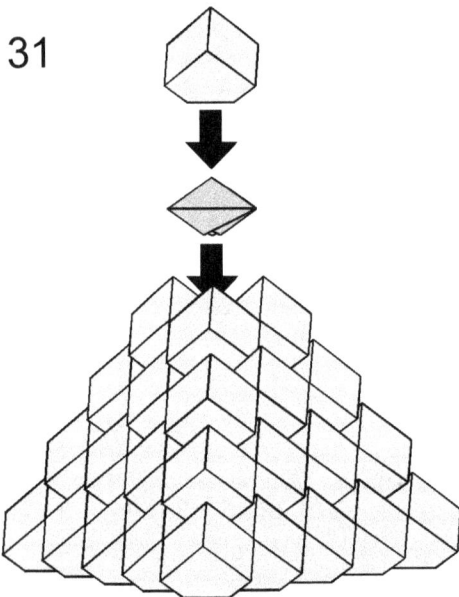

31. Complete the pyramid by dropping a single link unit into the hole in the top of the fourth tier and placing the last Columbus Cube on top.

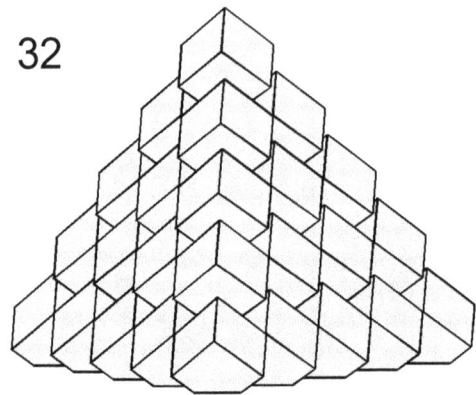

32. The five tier Columbus Pyramid is finished.

David Mitchell / Building with Butterflies

The Columbus Tower Revisited

Now that you know how to link Columbus Cubes into rows and tiers further sculptural possibilities emerge. You might also like to experiment with linking and stacking Tetracubes and other Columbus Cube variants in this way.

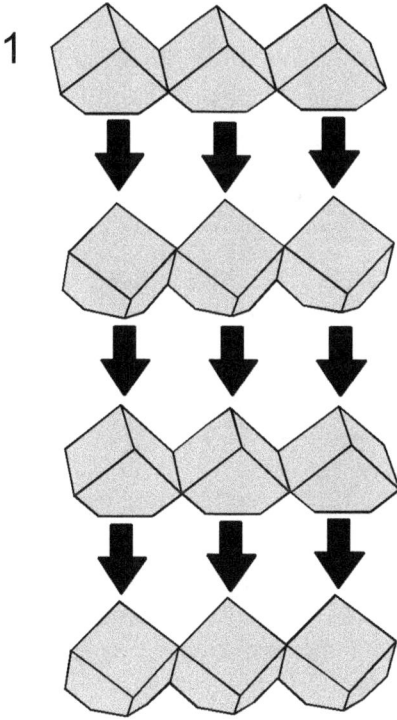

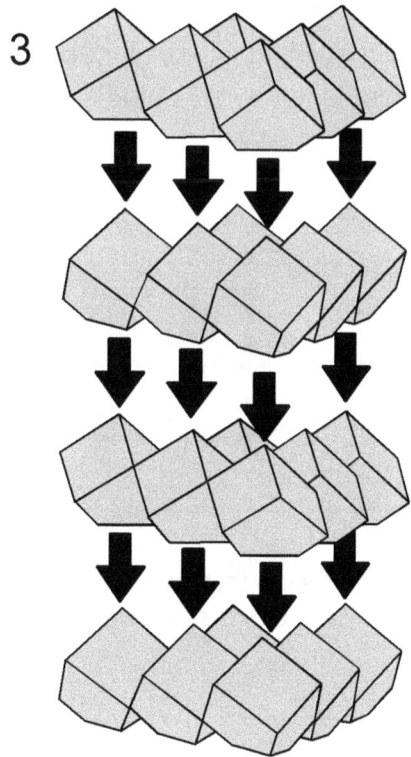

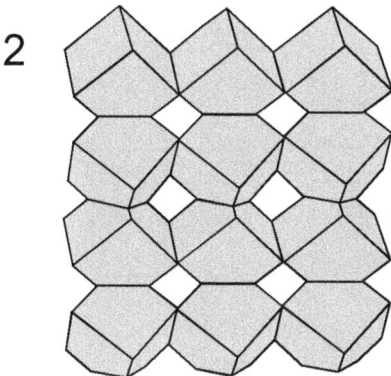

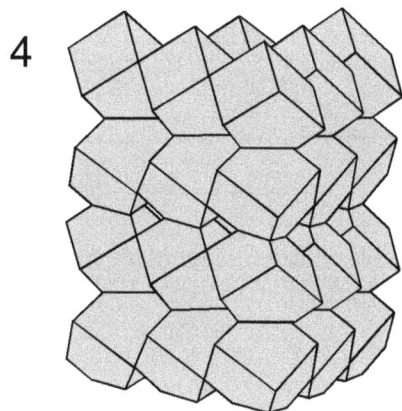

Ring of Cubes

Five Columbus Cubes will fit together to form a Ring of Cubes. The fit between the cubes isn't mathematically exact but it is good enough to fool the eye into thinking it might be. When I first discovered this I simply glued the cubes together, which works fine, but you might like to try the pure paperfolding method explained here.

You will need six squares of paper for each cube, so thirty squares in all. This design works best if you use medium weight paper. Begin by folding one square to step 9 of the Columbus Cube (see page 42).

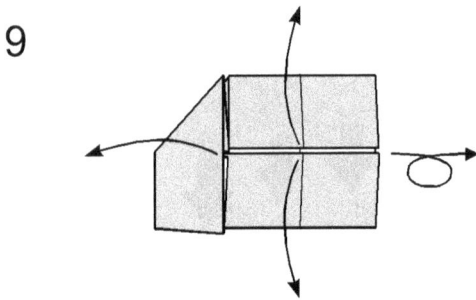

9. Arrange like this then open out completely and turn over sideways.

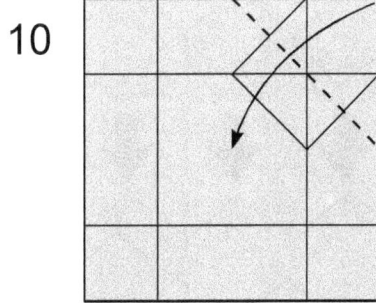

10. Fold the top right corner into the centre. You can do this accurately by lining up the creases in the way shown in picture 11.

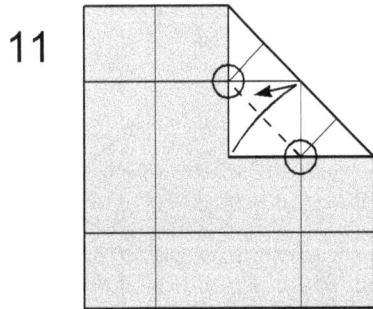

11. Fold the inside corner of the front flap outwards, then unfold.

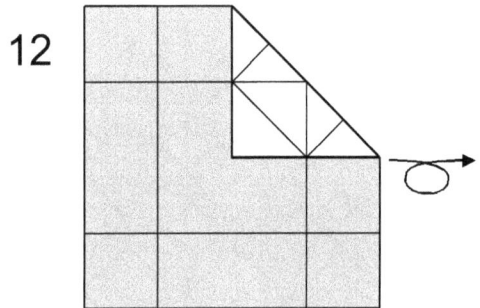

12. Turn over sideways.

David Mitchell / Building with Butterflies

13

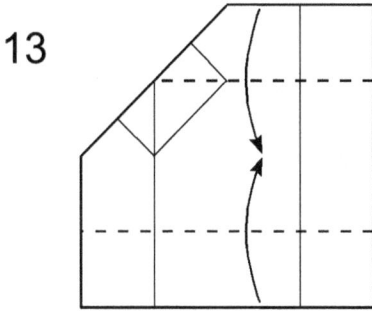

13. Fold the top and bottom edges inwards using the existing creases.

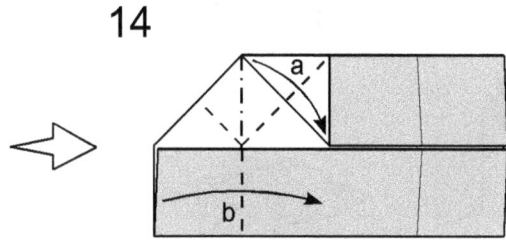

14

14. Make fold a then fold b. The result should look like picture 15.

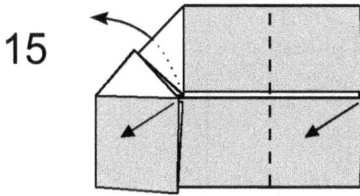

15

15. Lift both ends of the module towards you at right angles and swing the hidden flap into sight.

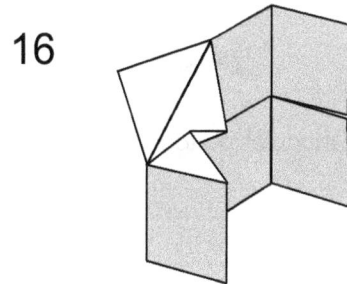

16

16. The first module is finished. You need to make four more like this.

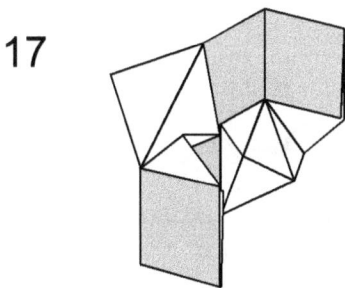

17

17. Turn one of the four through 180 degrees and follow steps 9 to 16 again to invert the opposite corner as well. The finished module will look like this.

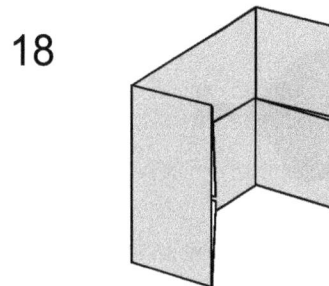

18

18. You will also need one standard module (see page 13).

19

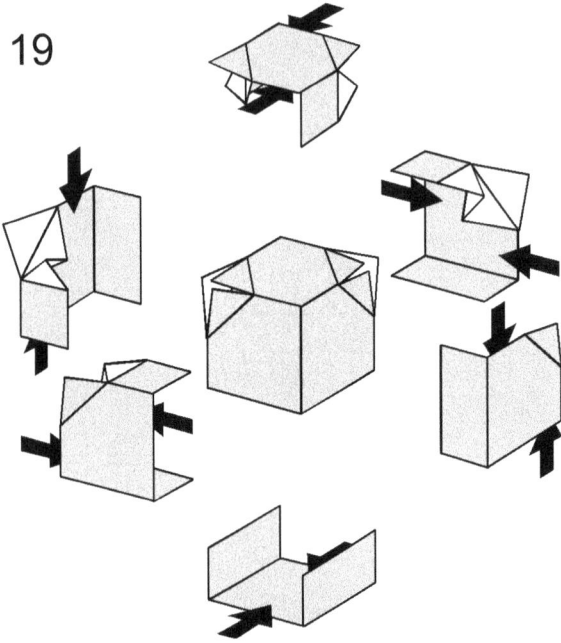

19. The six modules go together like this.

20

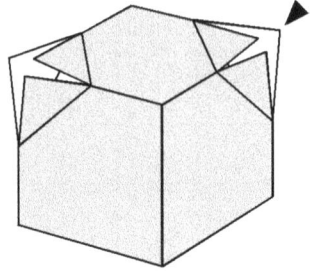

20. Push the tabs on one corner inwards.

21

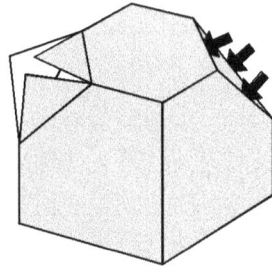

21. There are now three pockets around the edges of the inverted corner. Make five cubes like this.

22

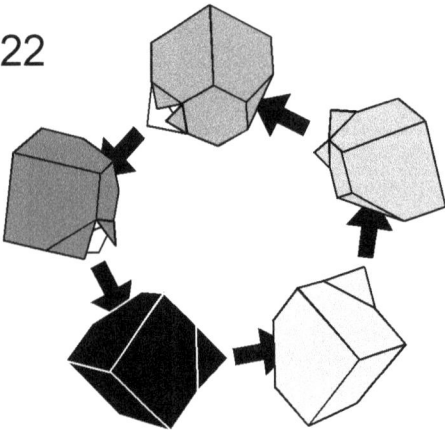

22. The tabs of one cube slide into the pockets of another.

23

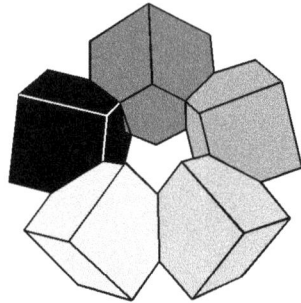

23. The Ring of Cubes is finished.

David Mitchell / Building with Butterflies

Ball of Cubes

The Ball of Cubes is made from twenty cubes (or more accurately from twenty macro-modules derived by inverting some of the corners of a cube). The method is essentially similar to that used for the Ring of Cubes except that three corners of each cube must be inverted to provide sufficient tabs and pockets to hold the Ball of Cubes together.

Each macro-module is made from six square sheets of paper. Medium weight paper works best.

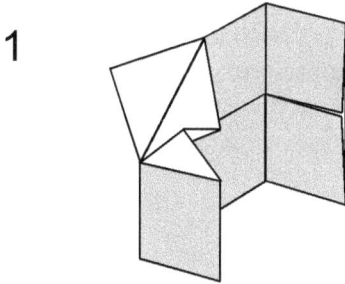

1. You will need three modules like this (see steps 1 to 16 of the Ring of Cubes).

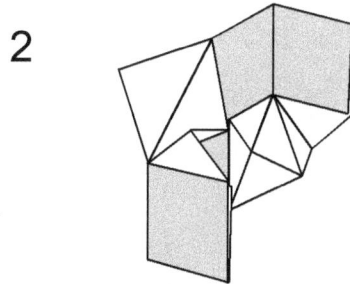

2. And three like this (see step 17 of the Ring of Cubes).

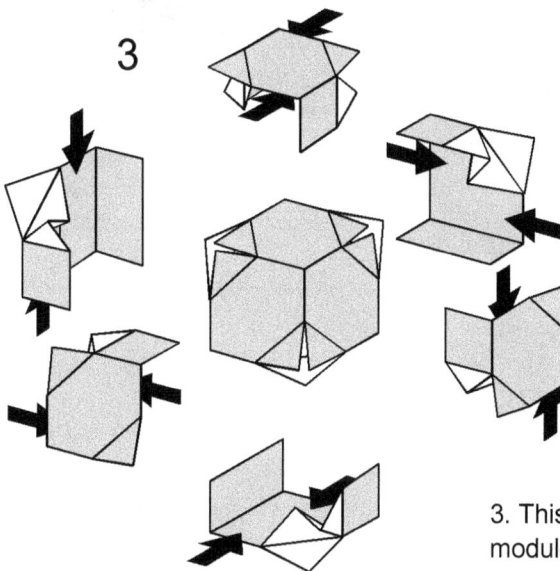

3. This is how the modules go together.

4

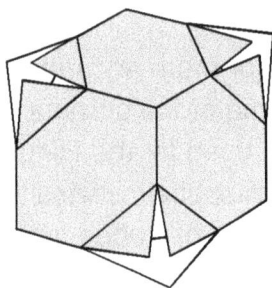

4. When first made each of the macro-modules should look like this.

5

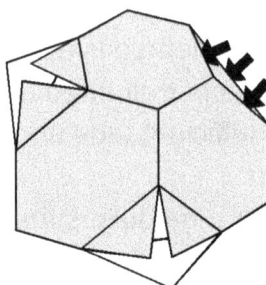

5. In order to assemble the Ball of Cubes you will need ten macro-modules where the tabs surrounding one inverted corner have been folded inwards to reveal the pockets like this ...

6

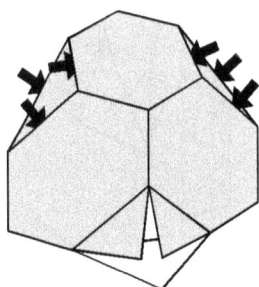

6. ... and ten where the tabs surrounding two inverted corners have been folded inwards like this. It is probably easiest to alter the macro-modules as you put them together rather than in advance. The Ball of Cubes is built by assembling successive rings of macro-modules to create a dodecahedral form.

7

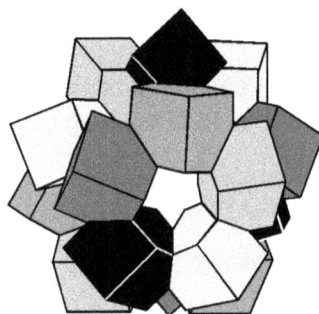

7. The finished Ball of Cubes looks like this. The example shown here is made from four cubes in each of five colours.

A mathematical footnote

Zsolt Lengvarsky has shown that the mathematical inaccuracy in the fit of the macro-modules in this design, and by extension in the design of the Ring of Cubes as well, can be overcome by a small alteration to the angles of the inversion. His calculations also yielded a second solution for a ball of twenty cubes which is totally different from mine.

David Mitchell / Building with Butterflies

The Icarus Tower

The corners of Icarus Cubes can be inverted using a similar method to that used to invert the corners of Paul Jackson's Cube. If just one corner is inverted the cubes can be stacked to create the Icarus Tower. The upper and lower wings of the macro-modules line up within the stack and joining pieces can be used to hold them together. This integrates the sculpture so that it can be handled as a unit.

You will need six modules for each cube. Three are standard Icarus Cube modules. Make the other three by following steps 1 to 10 of the Icarus Cube (see pages 55 and 56) then steps 11 to 15 below.

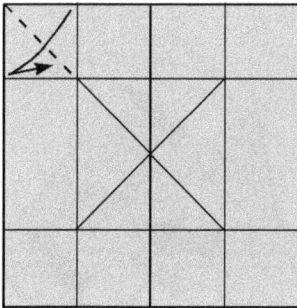

11. Extend the diagonal crease across the corner square.

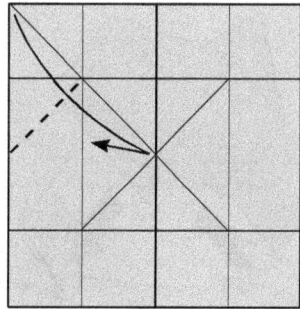

12. Fold the top left corner into the centre, then unfold, but only crease half way across the line of the fold.

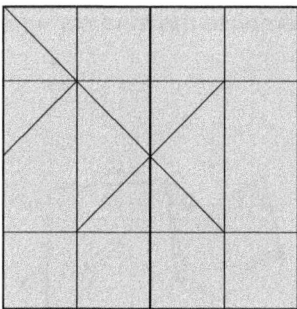

13. Turn over sideways.

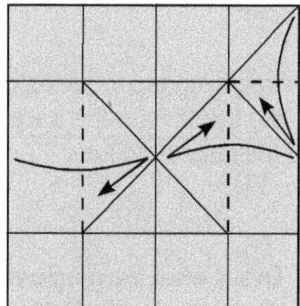

14. Reverse the direction of these three sections of crease.

15

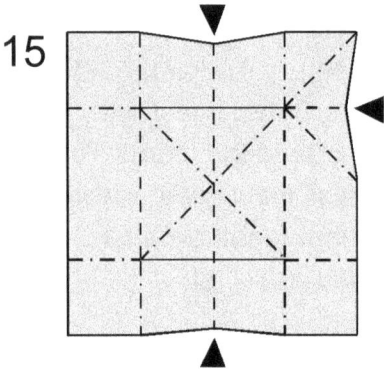

15. Collapse into shape so that the centre of the paper rises up towards you. The result should look like picture 16.

16

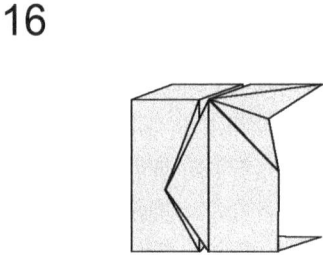

16. Make three. You will also need three standard Icarus Cube modules (see pages 55 to 57).

17

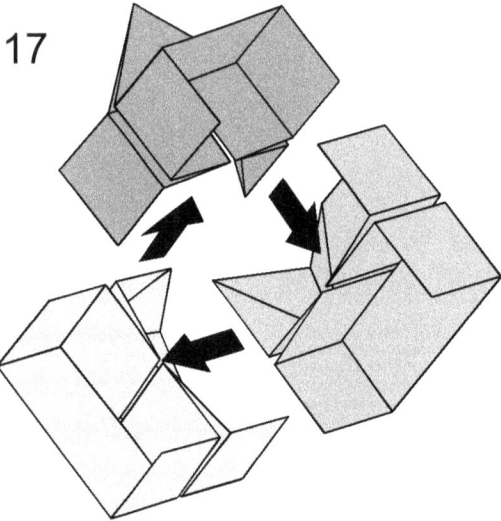

17. The three distorted modules go together like this to form the back corner of the macro-module.

18

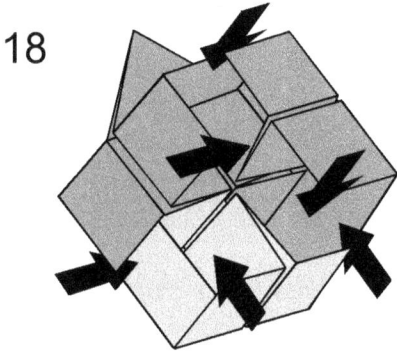

18. Add the standard modules one by one to complete the front corner as well.

19

19. This is what the macro-module should look like once the inverted corner has been rotated into sight. You will need four or five to make an Icarus Tower.

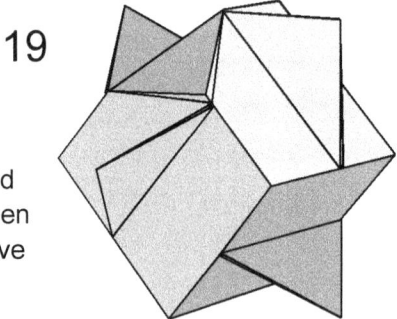

Making the joining pieces

You will need a square of the same size as the square you started from when making the modules (see page 55). If you are using irogami begin with the paper arranged white side up.

20

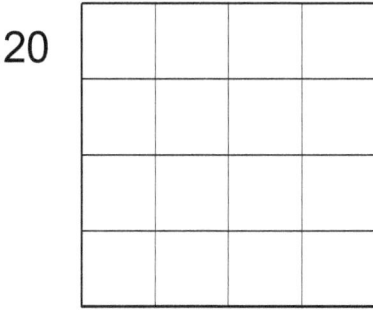

20. Begin by dividing the square into sixteen smaller squares with six creases like this.

21

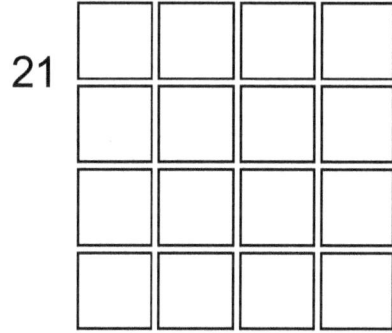

21. Separate the small squares by cutting along the horizontal and vertical creases.

22

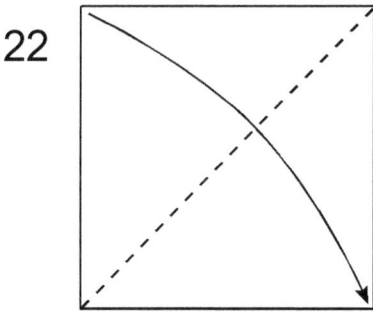

22. Fold one of the small squares diagonally in half.

23

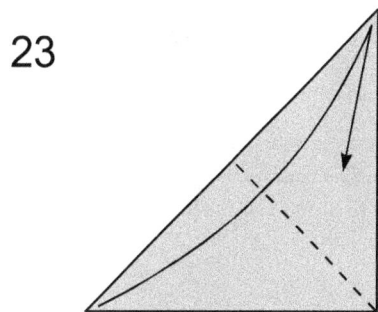

23. Fold in half diagonally again, then open most of the way out.

24

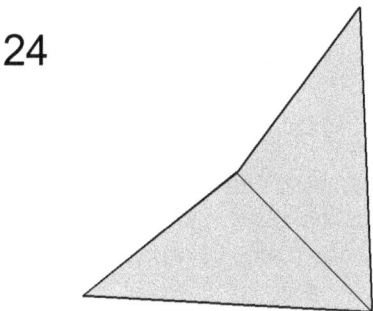

24. This is a joining piece. You will need twelve to hold together a five macro-module stack.

Assembling the Icarus Tower

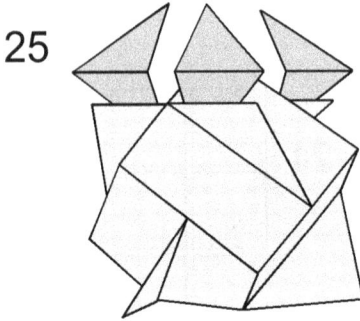

25

25. Stand one macro-module upright on the inverted corner and slide three joining pieces into the pockets in the upper edges of the wings.

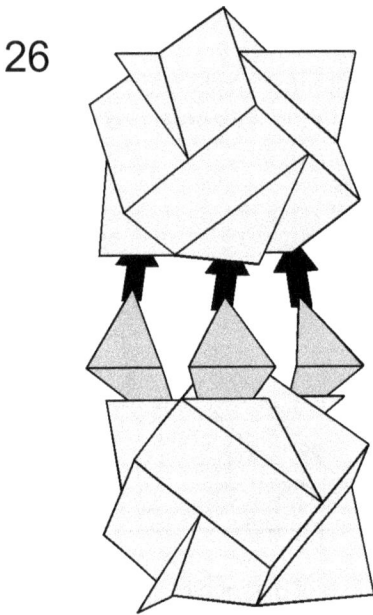

26

27

26. Add a second macro-module on top of the first by sliding the tops of the joining pieces into the pockets at the bottom of the lower wings. Push the macro-modules firmly together.

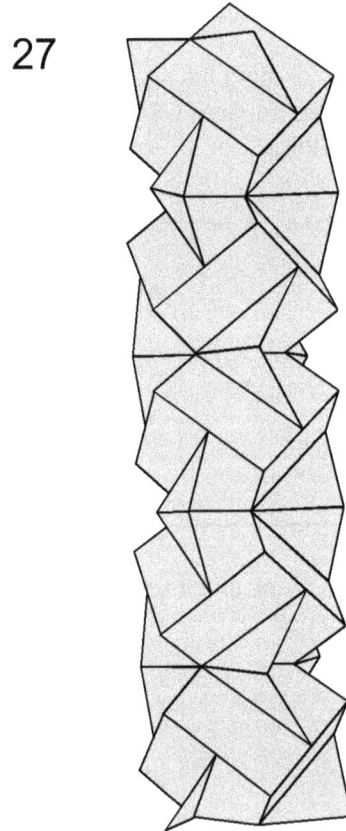

27. Continue to add macro-modules to the top of the stack in the same way. The finished Icarus Tower looks like this.

David Mitchell / Building with Butterflies

Building with Butterflies

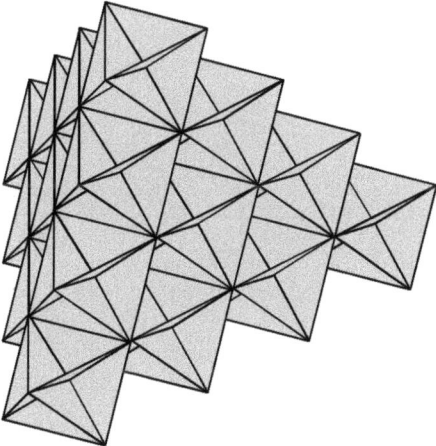

Building with Butterflies

The Modules

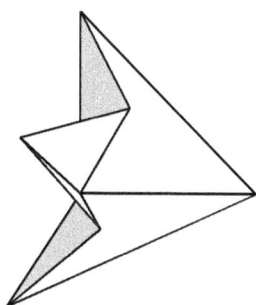

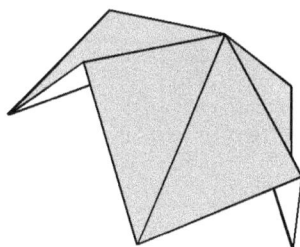

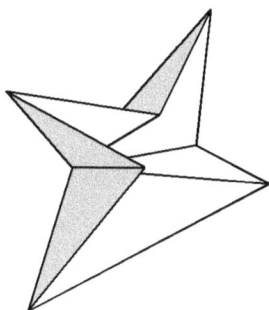

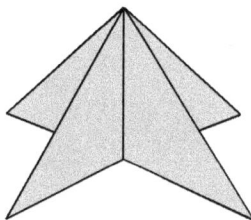

The Alpha Module

If you are using irogami begin white side up.

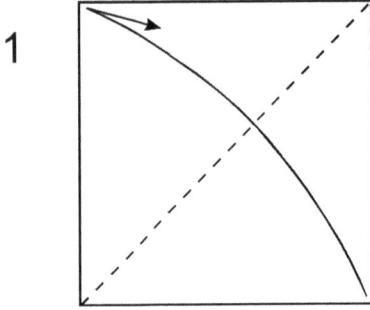

1. Fold in half diagonally, then unfold.

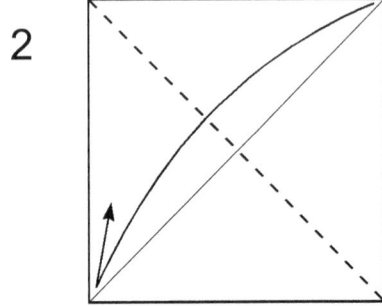

2. Fold in half diagonally in the other direction, then unfold.

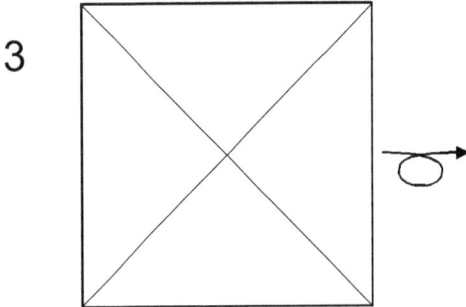

3. Turn over sideways.

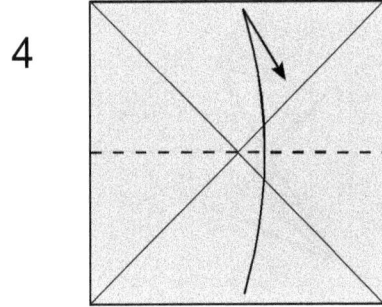

4. Fold in half upwards, then unfold.

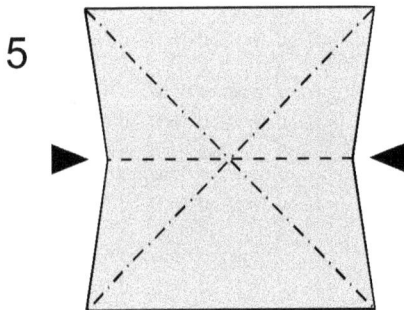

5. Collapse the module so that the centre rises up towards you.

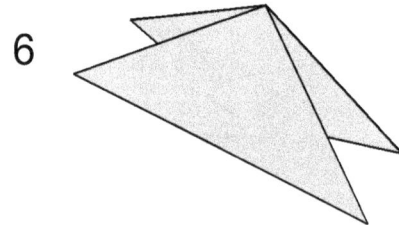

6. The Alpha module is finished. It is the most versatile of the modules and can be used to make the Alpha and Beta Prisms, the Twin Prisms, the Hybrid Prism, the Diamond Prism and the Alpha Cuboctahedron.

David Mitchell / Building with Butterflies

The Beta Module

If you are using irogami begin white side up.

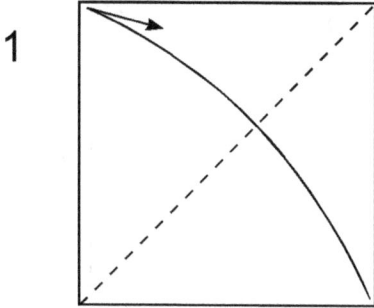

1

1. Fold in half diagonally, then unfold.

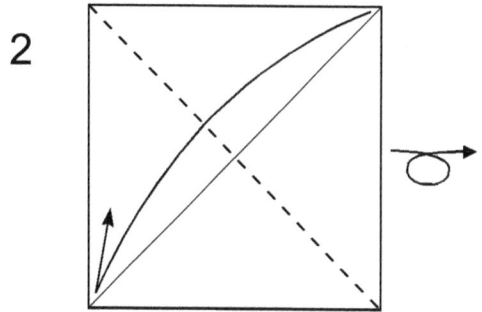

2

2. Fold in half diagonally in the other direction, then unfold. Turn over sideways.

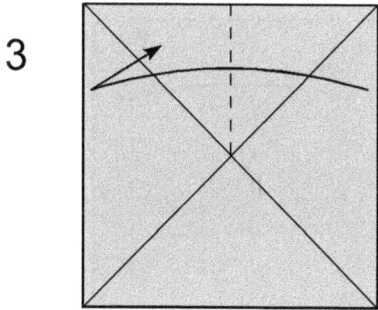

3

3. Fold in half sideways, then unfold, but only crease the top half of the paper.

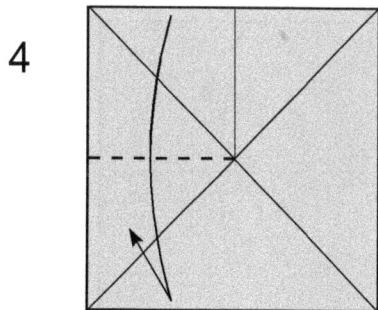

4

4. Make a similar fold across the left hand half of the paper by folding the paper in half upwards, then unfolding.

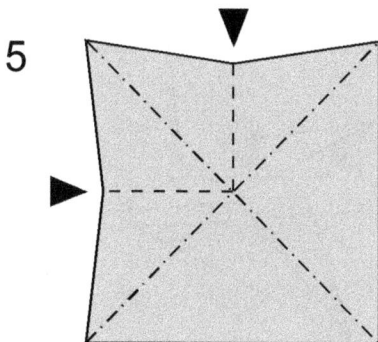

5

5. Collapse the module so that the centre rises up towards you.

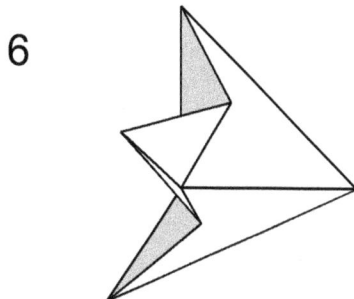

6

6. The Beta module is finished. It can be used to make the Beta Prism and the Diamond Prism.

The Gamma Module

If you are using irogami begin white side up.

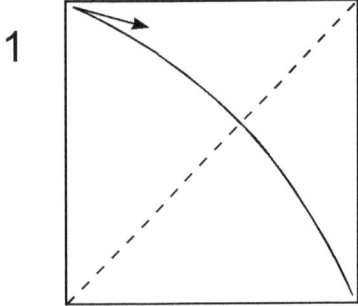

1. Fold in half diagonally, then unfold.

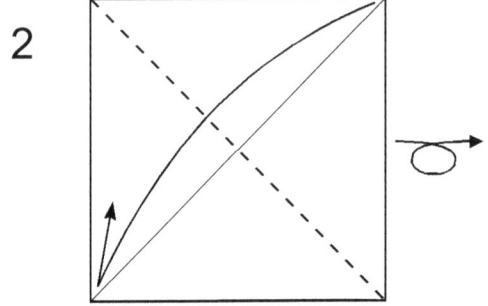

2. Fold in half diagonally in the other direction, then unfold. Turn over sideways.

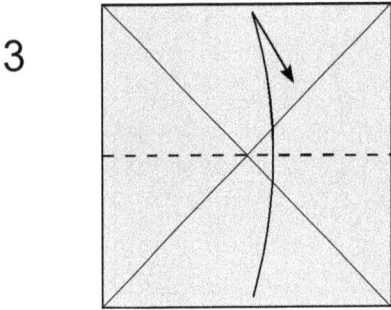

3. Fold in half upwards, then unfold.

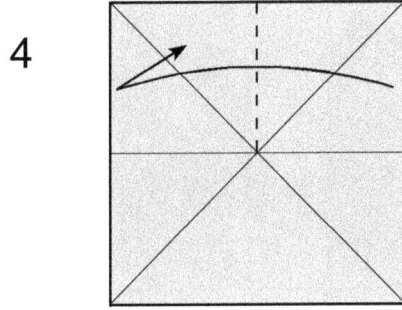

4. Fold in half sideways, then unfold, but only crease the top half of the paper.

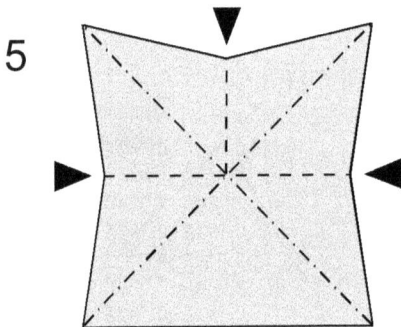

5. Collapse the module so that the centre rises up towards you.

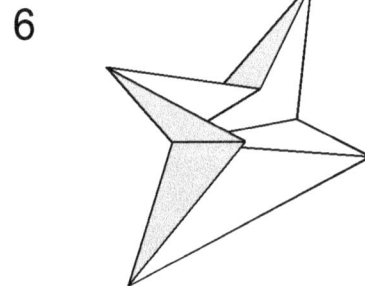

6. The Gamma module is finished. It can be used to make the Gamma Antiprism.

The Delta Module

If you are using irogami begin white side up.

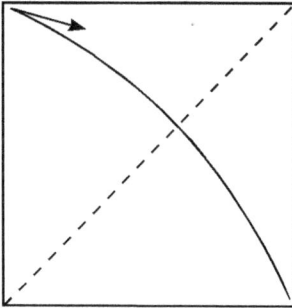

1. Fold in half diagonally, then unfold.

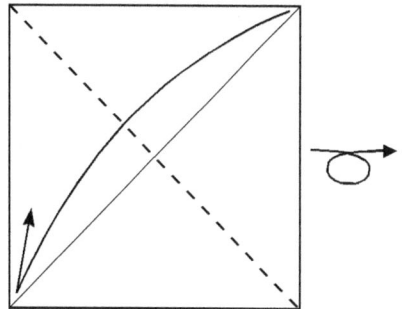

2. Fold in half diagonally in the other direction, then unfold. Turn over sideways.

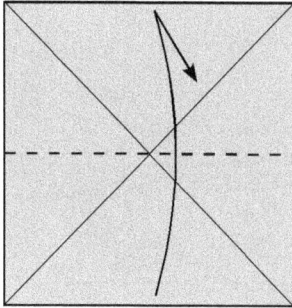

3. Fold in half upwards, then unfold.

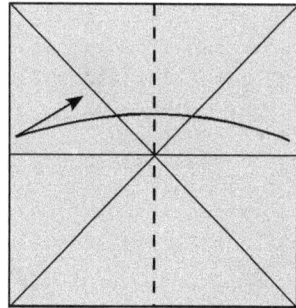

4. Fold in half sideways, then unfold.

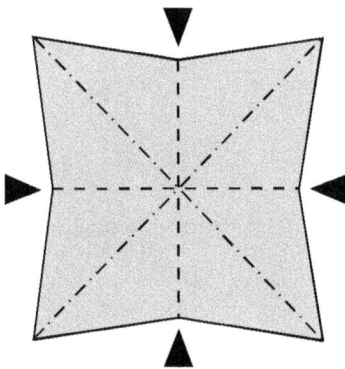

5. Collapse so that the centre rises up towards you.

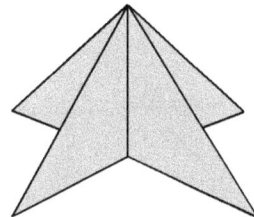

6. The Delta module, also known as the Waterbomb Base, is finished. This module can be used to make Robert Neale's Octahedron, the Rosebud Octahedron and the Hybrid Prism.

The Epsilon Module

If you are using irogami begin coloured side up.

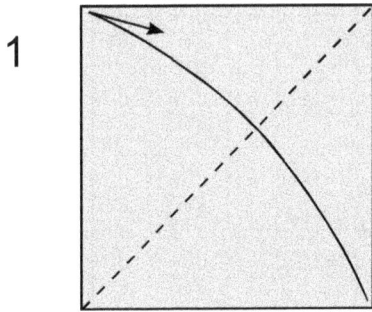

1

1. Fold in half diagonally, then unfold.

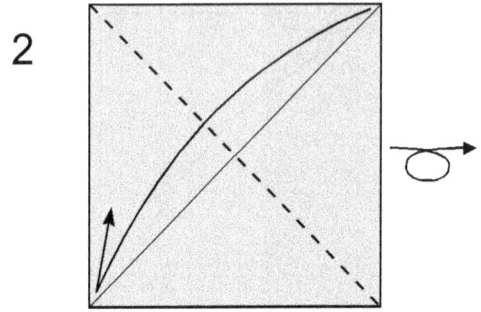

2

2. Fold in half diagonally in the other direction, then unfold. Turn over sideways.

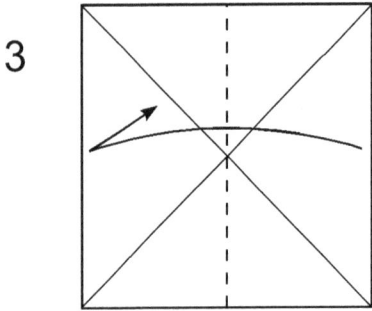

3

3. Fold in half sideways, then unfold.

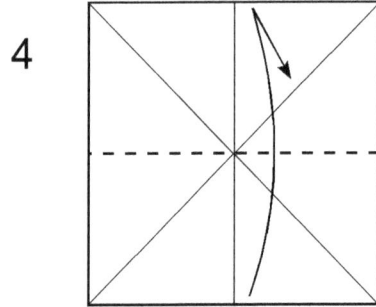

4

4. Fold in half upwards, then unfold.

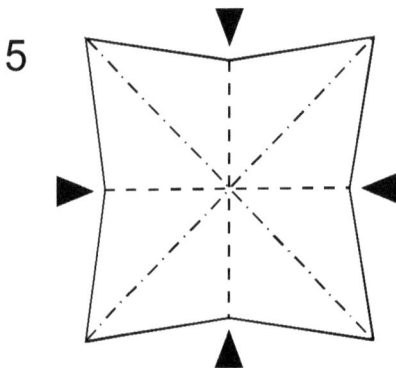

5

5. Collapse so that the centre moves away from you.

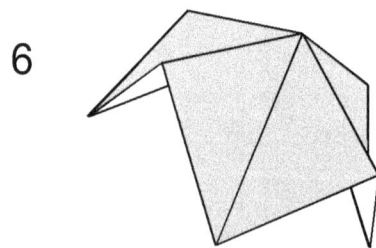

6

6. The Epsilon module, also known as the Preliminary Fold, is finished. It can be used to make the Epsilon Star and as a joining piece in the Sculptures section.

The Zeta Module

If you are using irogami begin white side up.

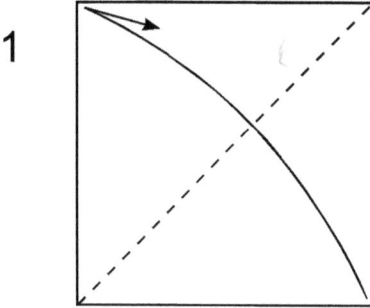

1

1. Fold in half diagonally, then unfold.

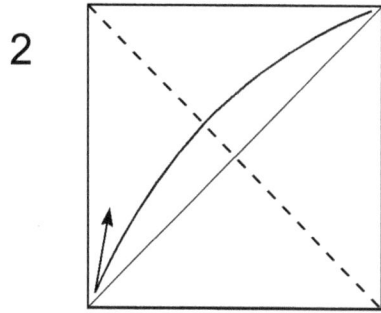

2

2. Fold in half diagonally in the other direction, then unfold.

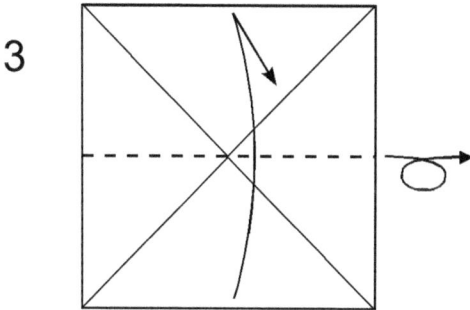

3

3. Fold in half upwards, then unfold. Turn over sideways.

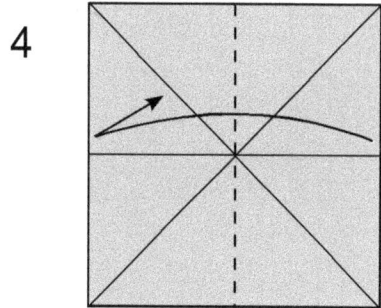

4

4. Fold in half sideways, then unfold.

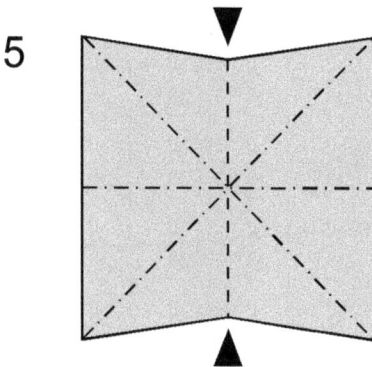

5

5. Collapse so that the centre of the paper rises up towards you.

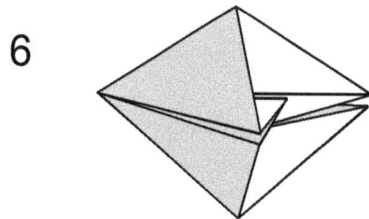

6

6. This is the result. The Zeta module can be used to make the Zeta Hexahedron.

Building with Butterflies

The Assemblies

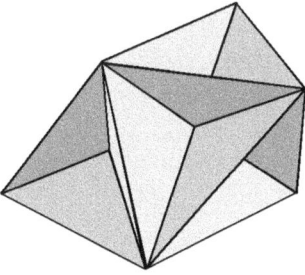

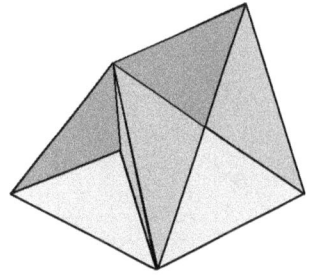

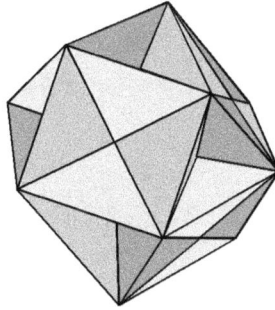

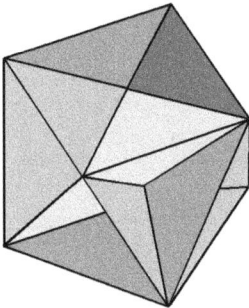

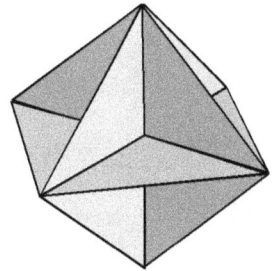

The Alpha Prism

1

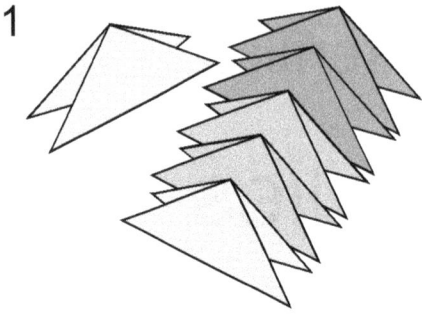

1. You will need six Alpha modules.

2

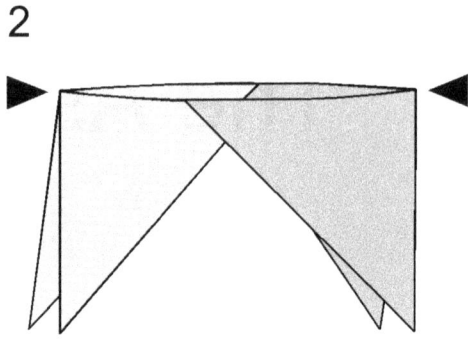

2. Interweave the arms of two modules like this and push them firmly together.

3

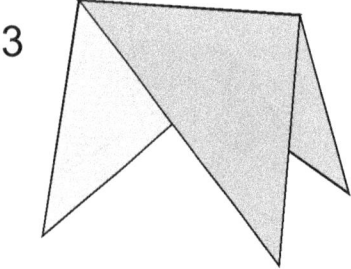

3. The two modules form a stable sub-assembly.

4

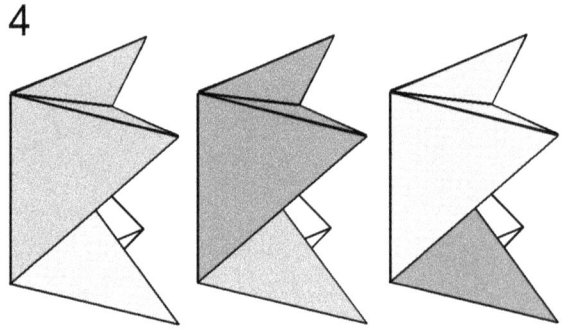

4. Make three sub-assemblies like this.

5

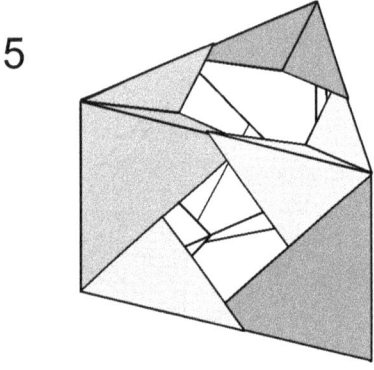

5. Interweave the tips of the arms of the sub-assemblies and push them together.

6

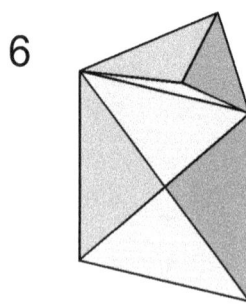

6. The finished Alpha Prism looks like this.

David Mitchell / Building with Butterflies

The Twin Prisms

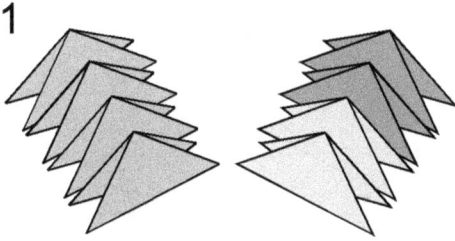

1

1. You will need eight Alpha modules.

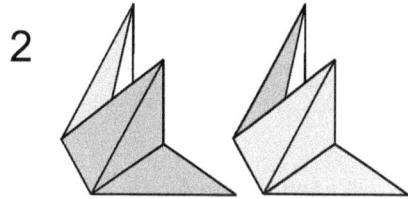

2

2. Begin by using four of the modules to make two sub-assemblies (see page 88).

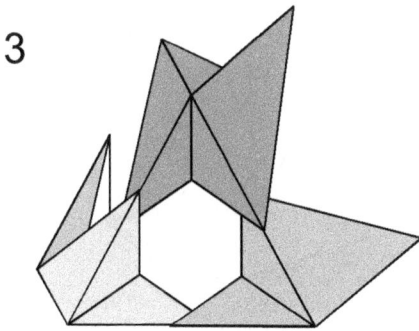

3

3. Add two further modules to one of the sub-assemblies. The design is not stable at this stage.

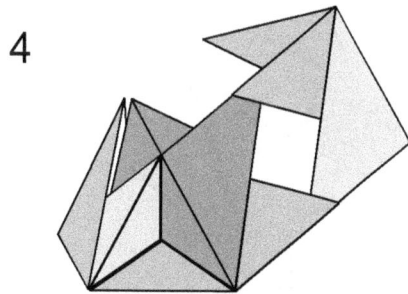

4

4. Add the second sub-assembly like this.

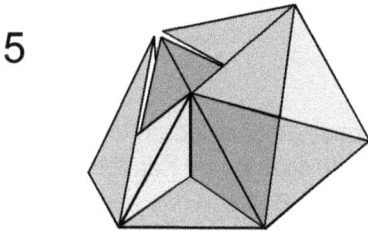

5

5. The remaining two modules are woven into the back of the assembly in the way shown in picture 3.

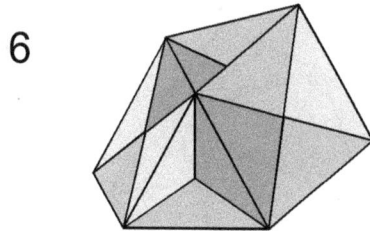

6

6. The Twin Prisms are finished.

The Alpha Cuboctahedron

1. You will need twelve Alpha modules.

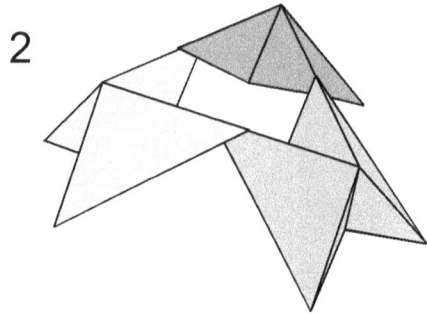

2. Three modules go together to form a triangular assembly like this.

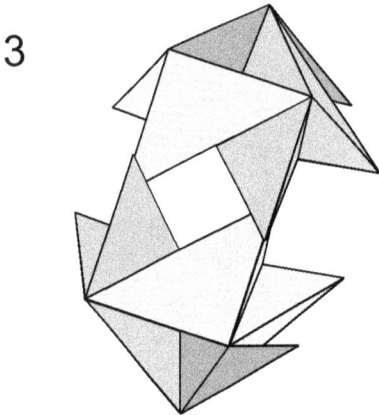

3. Two triangular assemblies can be combined to form one of the square faces.

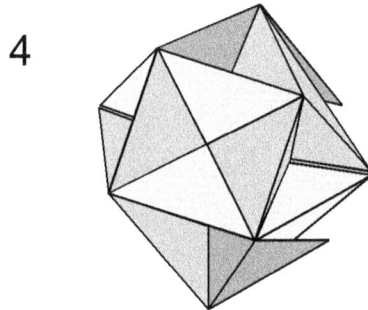

4. If you continue adding modules while keeping to the same pattern the assembly will form automatically. The assembly is not stable at first.

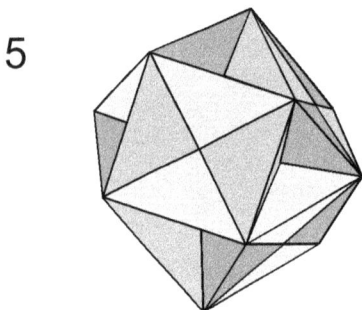

5. The finished Alpha Cuboctahedron looks like this. This form was first discovered by Kenneth Kawamura who calls it the Butterfly Ball and has used it as the basis of a fine piece of performance art. When tossed into the air and struck firmly with the open palm of one hand the ball will explode into its component modules which flutter to the ground. It is possible to increase the impact of this effect by hiding extra loose modules inside the ball.

The Beta Prism

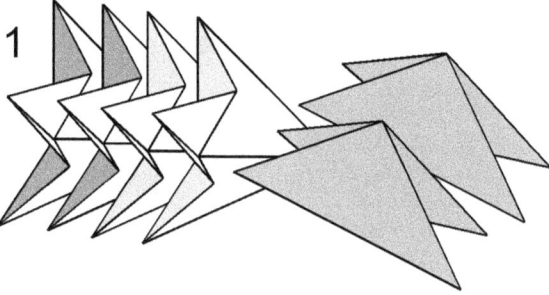

1. You will need two Alpha modules and four Beta modules.

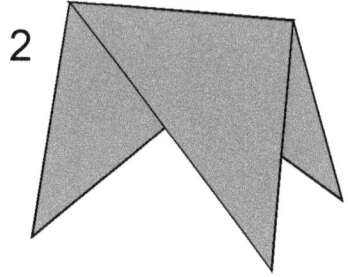

2. Begin by putting the Alpha modules together to form a sub-assembly (see page 88).

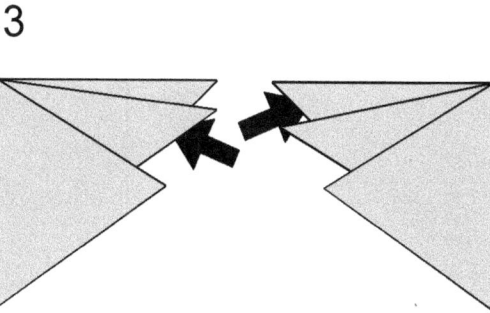

3. Each pair of Beta modules also go together to form a sub-assembly, like this.

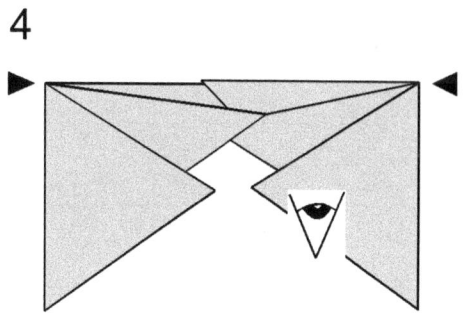

4. Push the modules firmly together. The next picture is drawn from a different viewpoint.

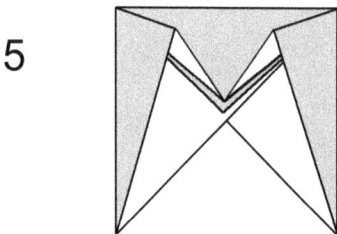

5. A finished Beta sub-assembly looks like this. Make two.

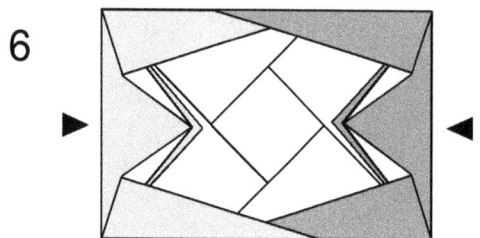

6. Interweave the two Beta sub-assemblies and slide them fully together.

7

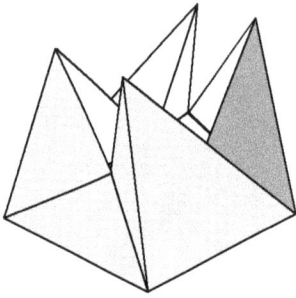

7. This is what the result should look like.

8

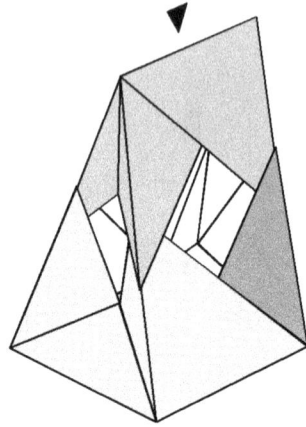

8. Add the Alpha sub-assembly, like this.

9

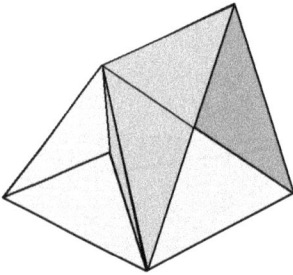

9. The Beta Prism is finished.

10

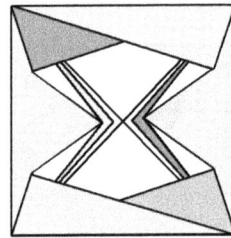

10, 11 and 12. These pictures show the same assembly sequence but using sub-assemblies which have each been made from modules of two different colours.

11

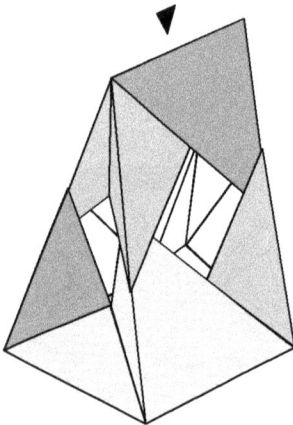

12

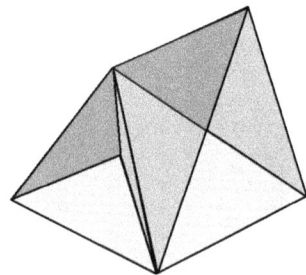

David Mitchell / Building with Butterflies

The Diamond Prism

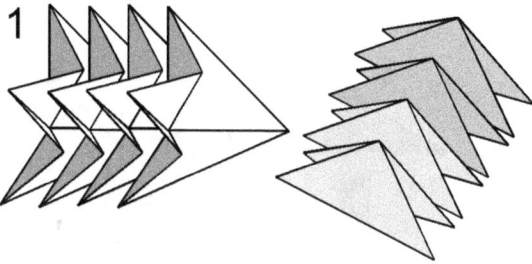

1. You will need four Alpha modules and four Beta modules.

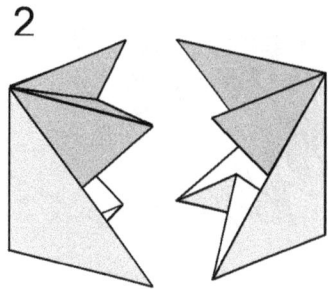

2. The Alpha modules go together to form two sub-assemblies (see page 88).

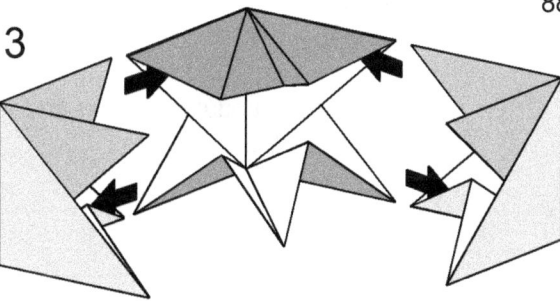

3. Add a pair of Beta modules to the Alpha sub-assemblies like this.

4. The arrows show how the remaining Beta modules fit into place.

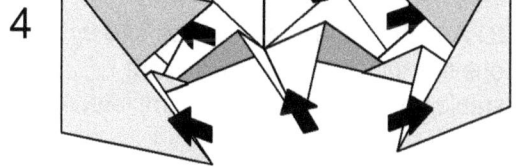

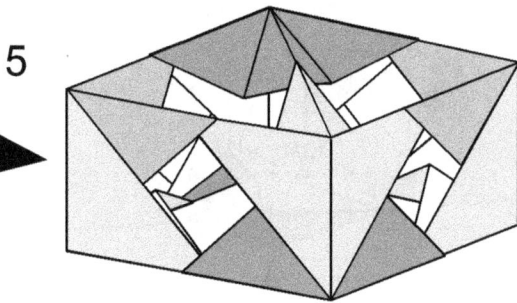

5. Arrange all the modules loosely like this then slide them together.

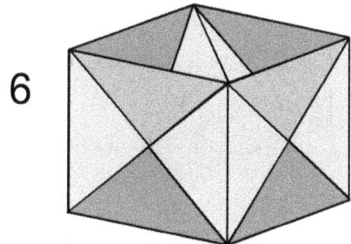

6. The Diamond Prism is finished.

The Gamma Antiprism

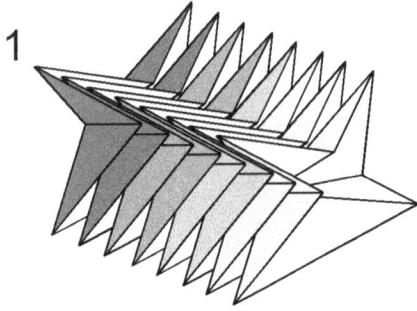

1

1. You will need eight Gamma modules.

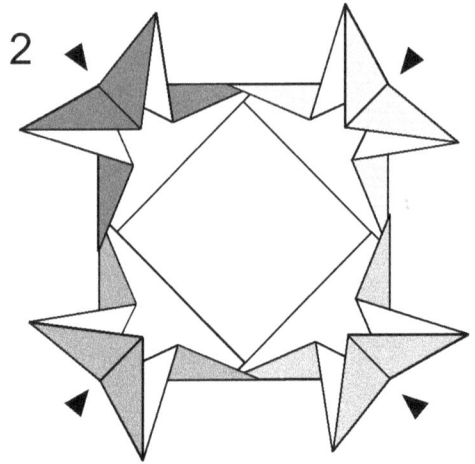

2

2. Arrange four modules like this and slide them together.

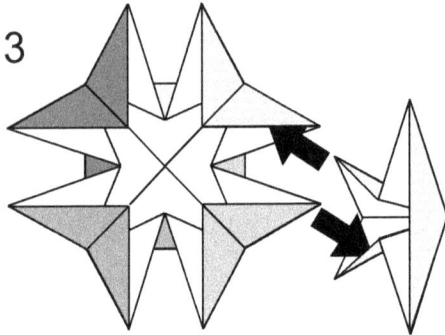

3

3. Add the remaining modules one by one like this. The assembly is not stable until the antiprism is complete.

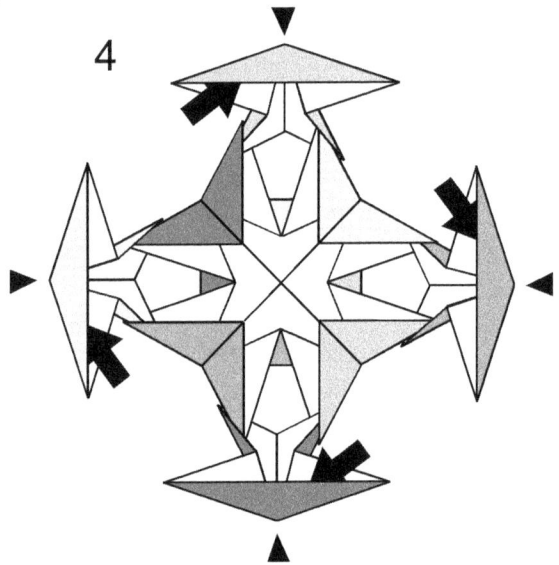

4

4. Weave the free arms of the modules together to form the top surface of the antiprism. Gradually ease all the modules fully into place.

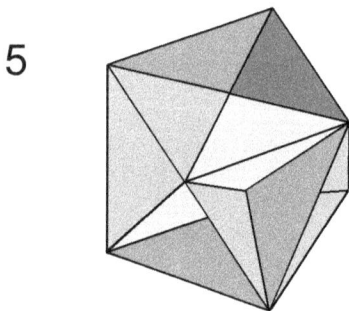

5

5. The Gamma Antiprism is finished.

Robert Neale's Octahedron

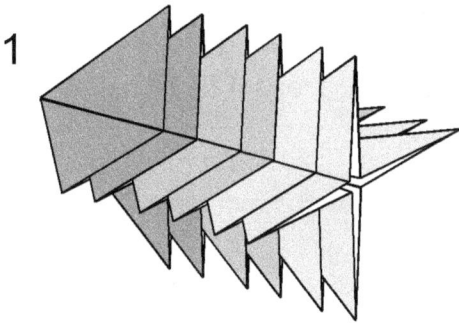

1

1. You will need six Delta modules.

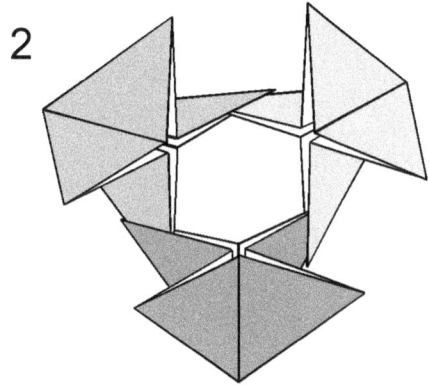

2

2. The first three modules are interwoven like this.

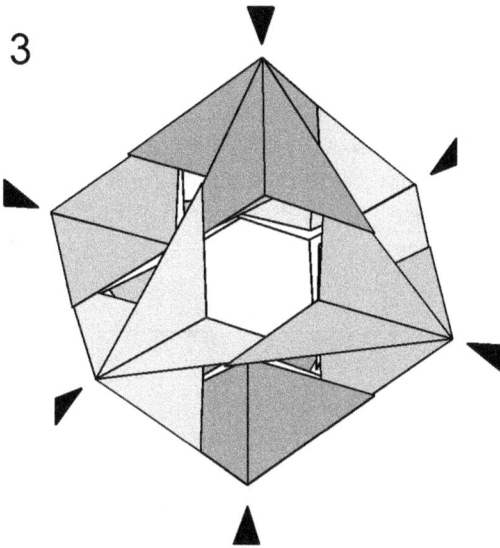

3

3. Add the remaining modules one by one, making sure that you maintain the weave pattern in the way shown here. When all the modules are in place gently ease them together until they lock firmly in place.

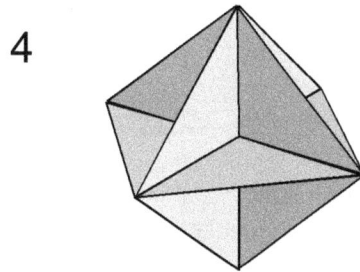

4

4. Robert Neale's Octahedron is finished. This design is one of the real treasures of modular origami.

The Rosebud Octahedron

The Rosebud Octahedron is a simple but subtle variation of Robert Neale's Octahedron. It is made from three Delta modules and three custom modules. Fold the custom modules by following steps 1 and 2 of the Delta module (see page 83) then follow steps 4 to 10 below.

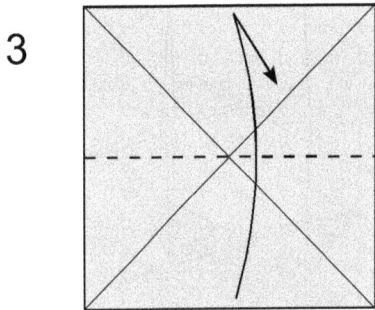

3. Fold in half upwards, then unfold.

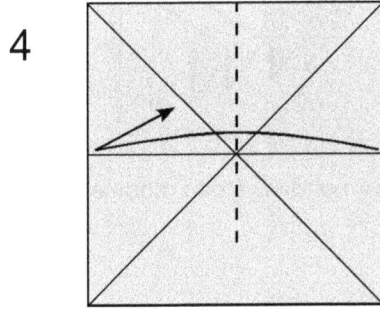

4. Fold in half sideways, then unfold, but only crease part way down the paper. The lowest point of the crease you make here should ideally intersect exactly with the crease you make in step 6. It is better to err by creasing too short rather than too far at first.

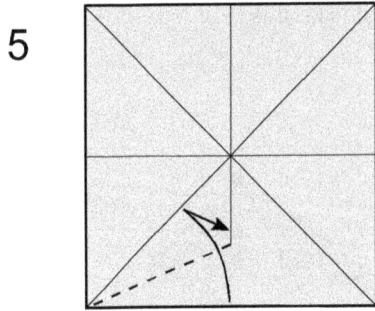

5. Fold the left hand half of the bottom edge onto the diagonal crease above it, then unfold. Only crease as far as the vertical centre crease.

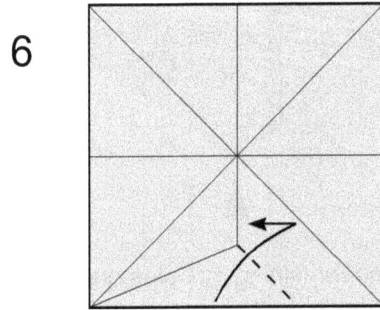

6. Make a crease parallel to the diagonal to link the point where the creases made in steps 5 and 6 intersect to the bottom edge.

7

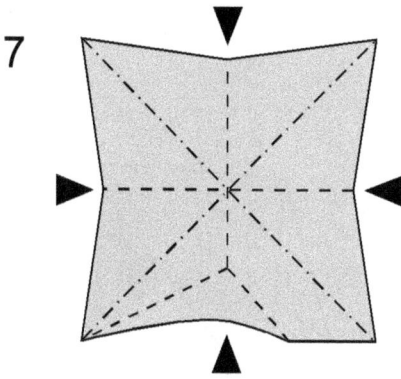

7. Collapse so that the centre of the paper rises up towards you.

8

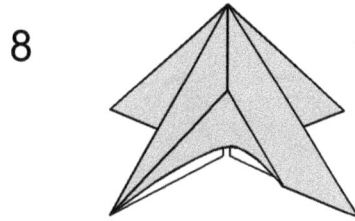

8. This is the custom module. The edge of the flap nearest to you should be curved.

9

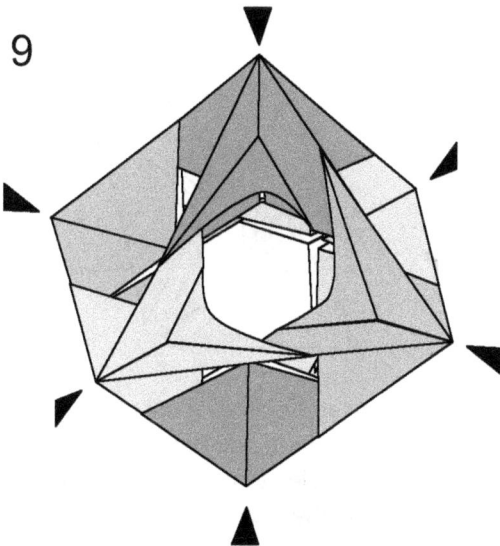

9. Assemble the modules in the same way as for Robert Neale's Octahedron (see page 95).

10

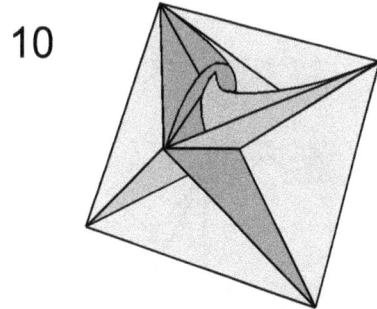

10. The finished result should look like this.

11

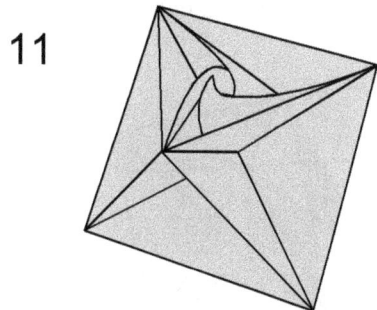

11. The design probably looks best when made in a single colour.

The Hybrid Prism

1

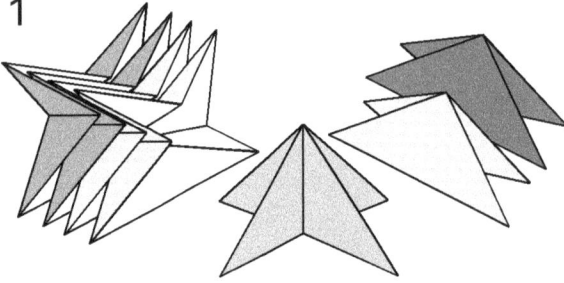

1. You will need two Alpha modules, four Gamma modules and one Delta module.

2

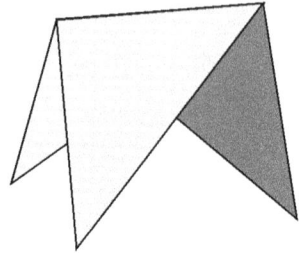

2. The Alpha modules go together to form a sub-assembly (see page 88).

3

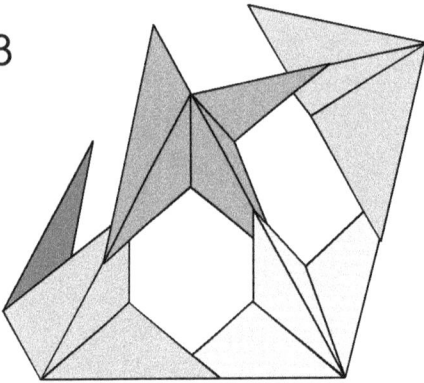

3. Add two of the Gamma modules to the sub-assembly like this, then add the Delta module to the right hand side.

4

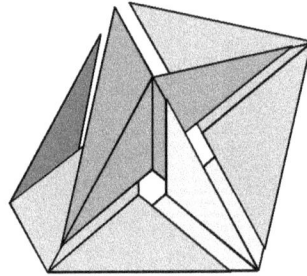

4. Ease these modules most of the way together then add the remaining Gamma modules to the far side of the assembly in the way shown in picture 3 opposite.

5

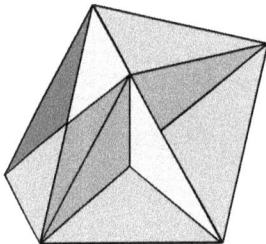

5. The finished Hybrid Prism looks like this.

6

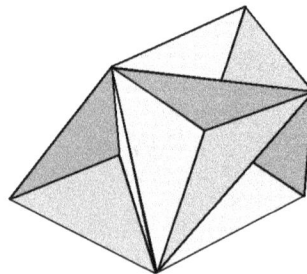

6. This is a view from another angle.

David Mitchell / Building with Butterflies

The Epsilon Star

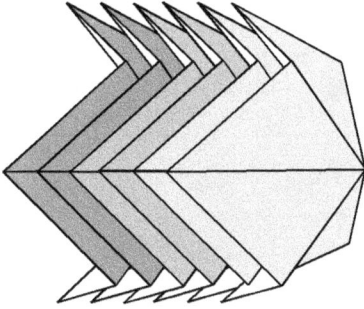

1. You will need six Epsilon modules.

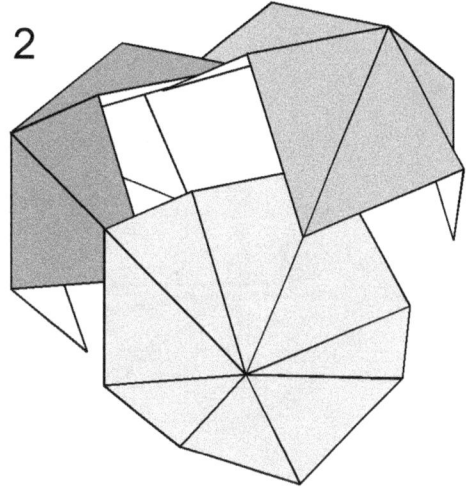

2. Begin by putting three modules together like this. Although the pictures show the modules in an exploded view for clarity you will need to slide them completely together.

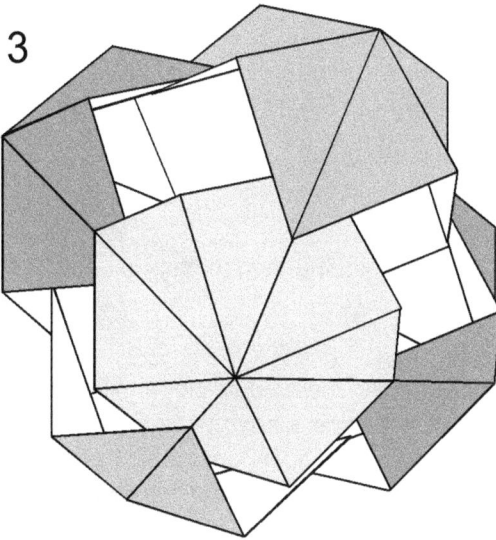

3. Add further modules until the star is complete. Note the way that the modules are woven together so that two opposite arms of each module go on the outside of other modules while the other two opposite arms go on the inside.

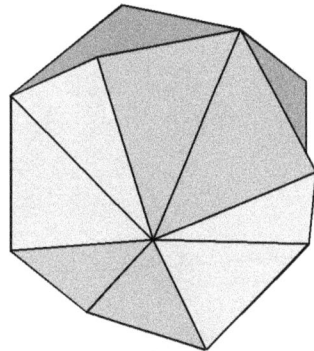

4. When you have succeeded in getting all six modules to nestle in place the Epsilon Star will look like this. The design is quite stable in its finished state.

The Zeta Hexahedron

1

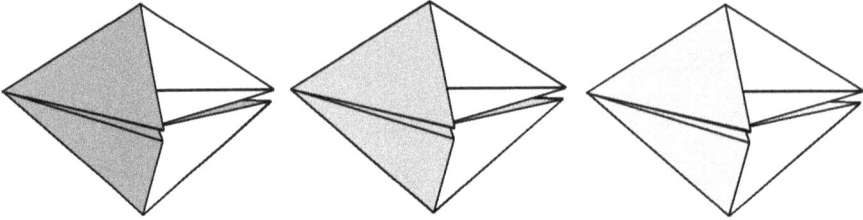

1. You will need three Zeta modules.

2

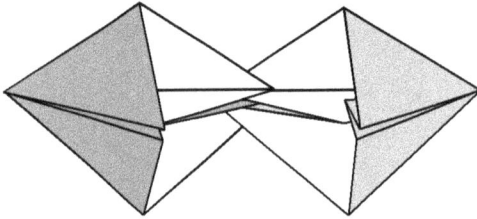

2. Arrange two modules so that the top and bottom halves of the back edges are interwoven in the way shown here.

3

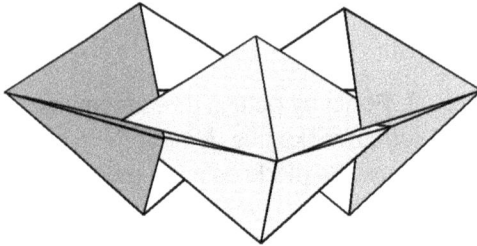

3. Add the third module like this.

4. Before pushing the modules together make sure the internal flaps are arranged like this. The set of flaps marked a push together in front, the set marked c go at the back and the set marked b lie in the middle.

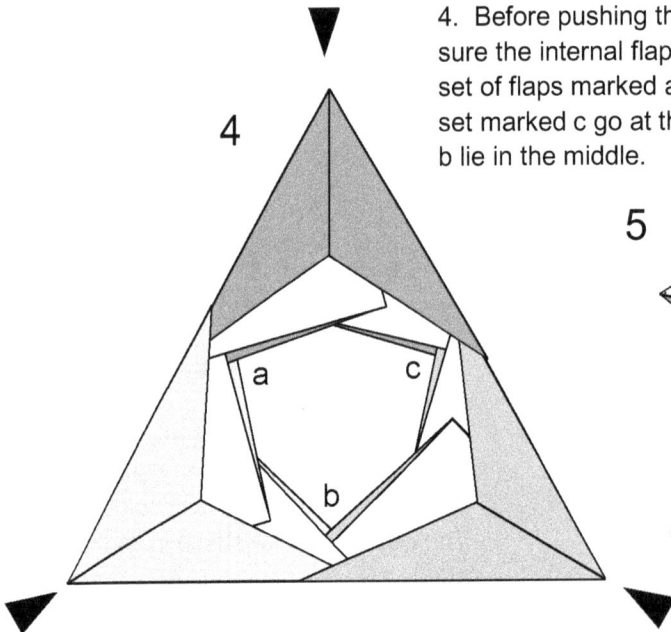

4

a   c

b

5

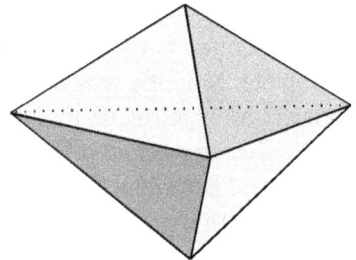

5. The Zeta Hexahedron is finished.

David Mitchell / Building with Butterflies

Building with Butterflies
The Sculptures

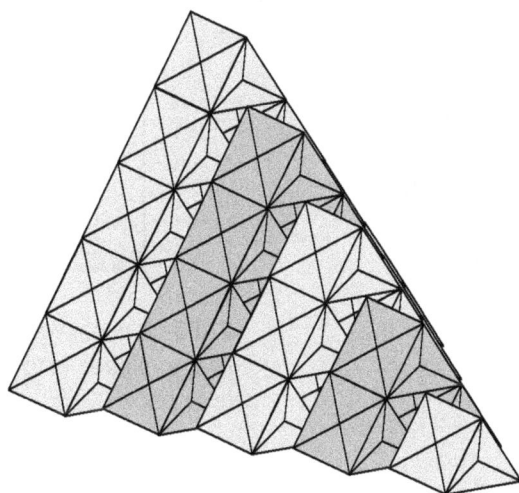

Alpha Pyramids

Alpha Prisms can be combined into Alpha Pyramids. The finished pyramids can in turn be combined into larger sculptures.

Alpha Prisms can be joined together in two quite different ways. The method I prefer, because of its simplicity, is just to use quarter size squares as joining pieces. However it is also possible to avoid the use of most of the joining pieces by turning some of the pockets into tabs. Where a joining piece is still necessary this can be made from a square of paper the same size as those used for the other modules. Both methods work equally well.

1
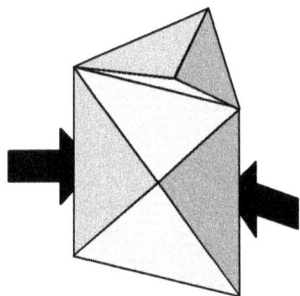

1. There are pockets in each of the long edges of the Alpha Prism.

2
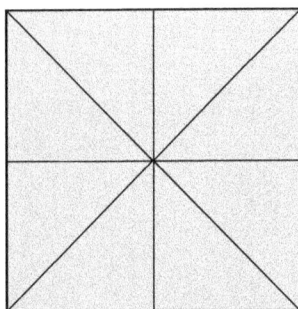

2. The easiest way to make the simple joining pieces is to fold a Delta module (see page 83) ...

3
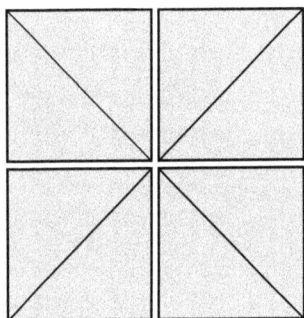

3. ... and cut it into quarters.

4
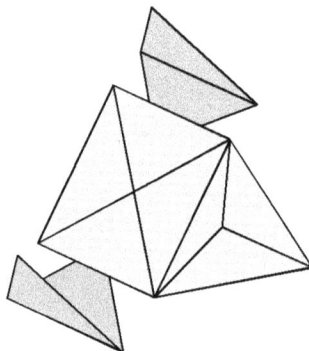

4. The tabs slide into the pockets like this.

5

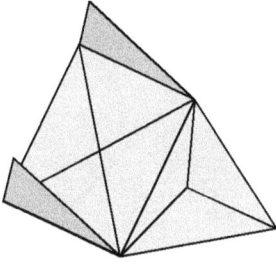

5. You can angle the joining pieces to make it easy to add other prisms.

6

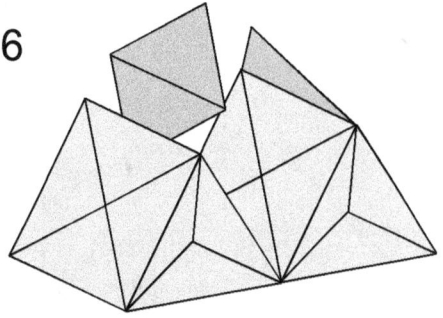

6. Once the second prism is in place add another joining piece.

7

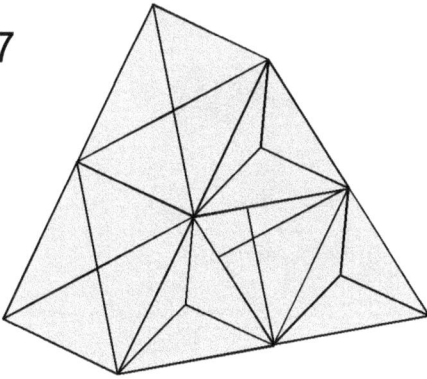

7. Slide a third prism onto the top. The simplest Alpha Pyramid is finished.

8

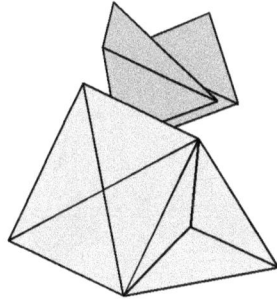

8. When building larger pyramids, you will need to use two joining pieces in the top of each internal prism.

9

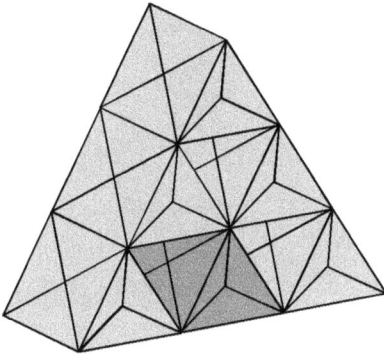

9. This is the six prism pyramid. The internal prism is the darker one.

10

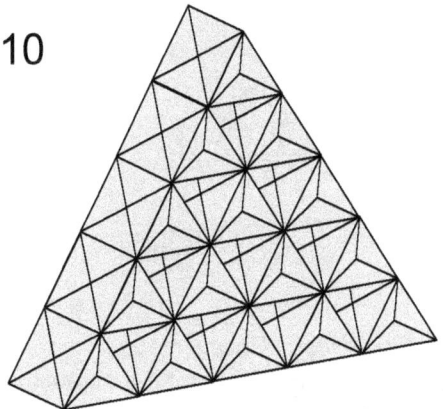

10. You can build Alpha Pyramids with many more layers in a similar way.

11

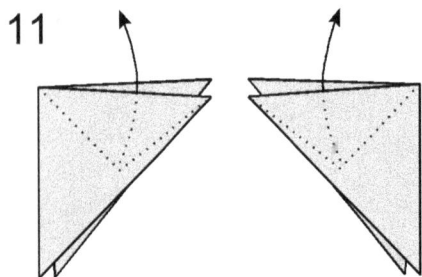

11. To turn a pocket into a tab separate one sub-assembly from the others, take the modules apart and pull out the internal flaps.

12

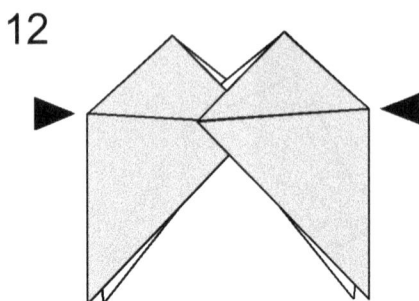

12. Interweave the layers of the modules and slide the sub-assembly back together.

13

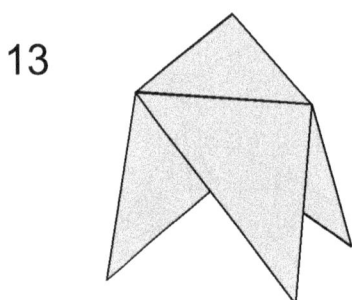

13. The sub-assembly will now look like this.

14

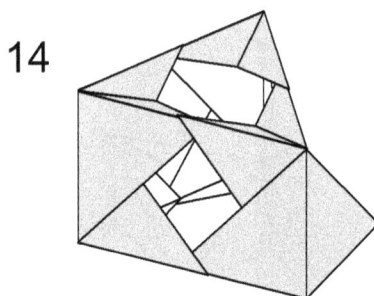

14. Put the sub-assemblies back together.

15

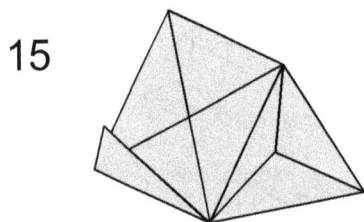

15. Three Alpha Prisms made in this way will go together to form a pyramid without the need for any joining pieces. For larger pyramids you will still need to use joining pieces at the top of the internal prisms.

16

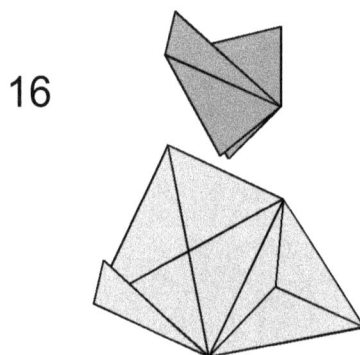

16. An Epsilon module folded from a full size square (see page 84) can be used as a joining piece at the top of the internal prisms.

David Mitchell / Building with Butterflies

Alpha Pyramids made from differing numbers of Alpha Prisms can be arranged to create third generation sculptures like this.

17

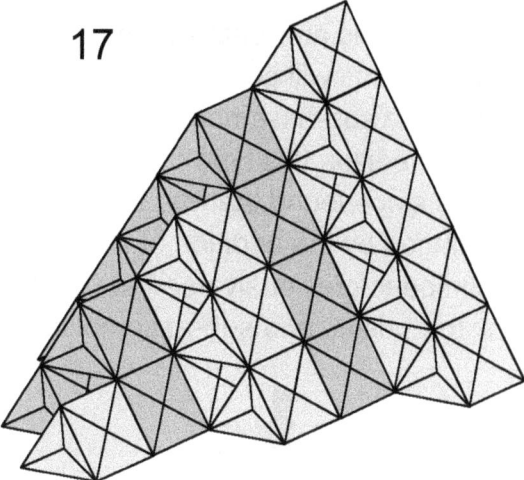

18

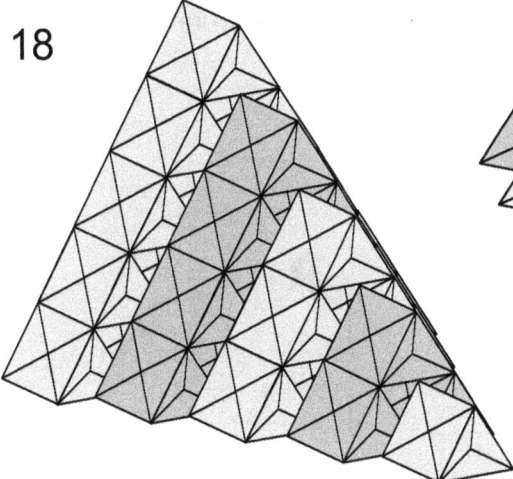

19

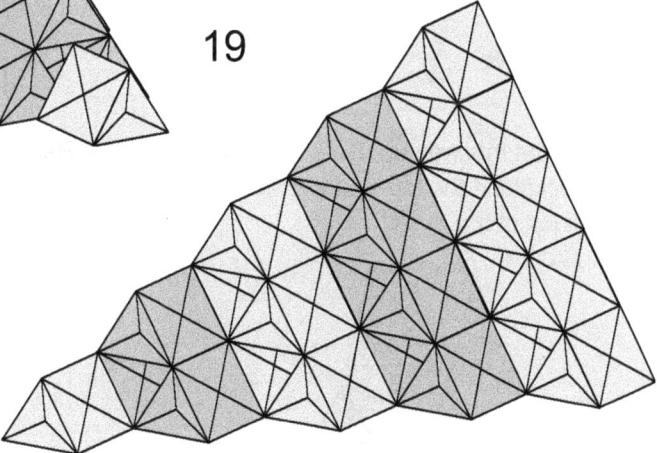

20

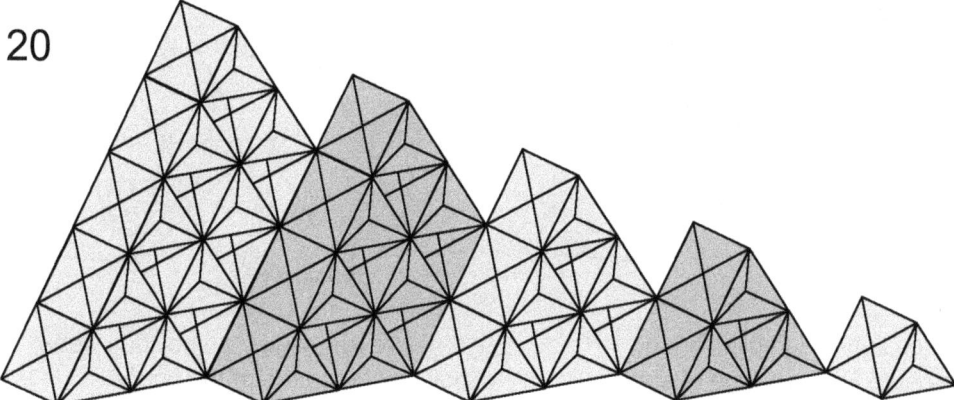

Damocles

Alpha Prisms and Beta Prisms can be combined to create Damocles. Three prisms will go together to form a macro-modular sub-assembly and these sub-assemblies can in turn be built into larger structures. In the first edition this type of structure was called the Tower of Babel. I have since found that the structure can be strengthened and enhanced by the addition of inverted Alpha Pyramids. Either of the techniques previously used to combine Alpha Prisms can be used to link the prisms and sub-assemblies together here.

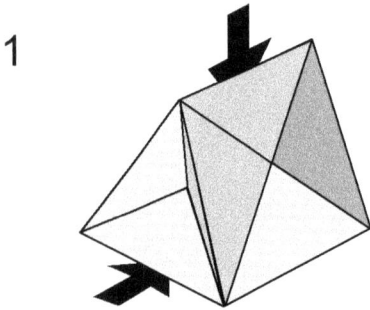

1. When sat this way up, Beta Prisms have pockets in the top and in both short sides of the base.

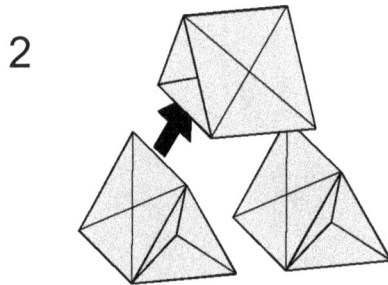

2. A Beta Prism can be stacked on top of two Alpha Prisms to form a sub-assembly.

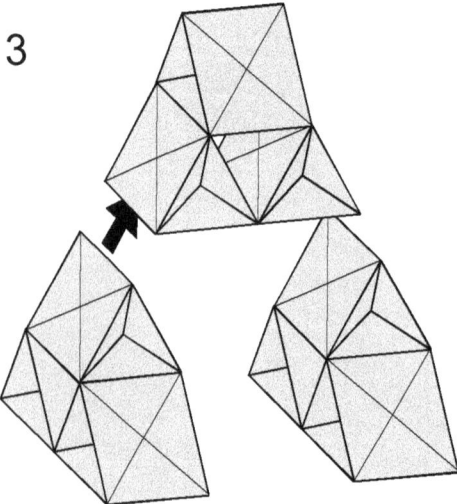

3. Three sub-assemblies will go together to form a bridge of sub-assemblies.

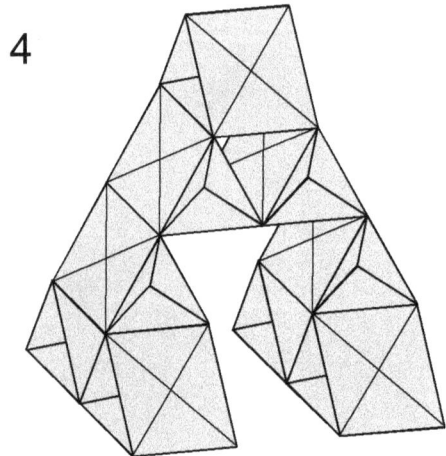

4. There is however an obvious weak point in the centre of the bridge.

5

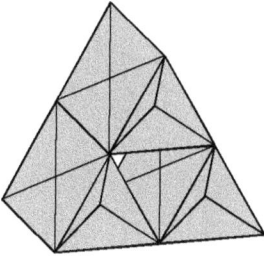

5. To address this weakness, first make a three prism Alpha Pyramid ...

6

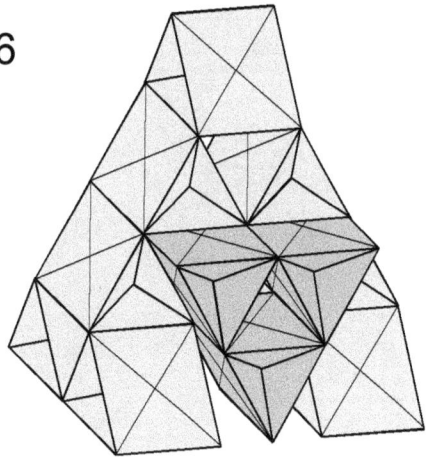

6. ... then turn it upside down and slide it into the hole underneath the bridge.

7

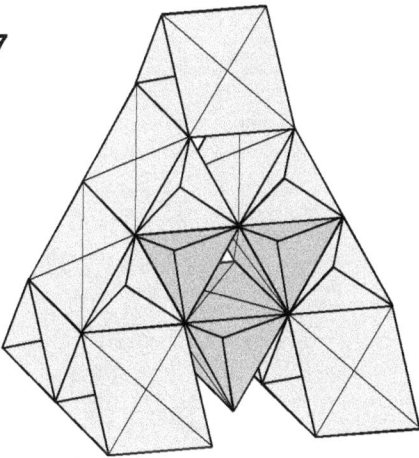

7. In a structure of this size the bottom point of the inverted Alpha Pyramid rests on the ground.

8

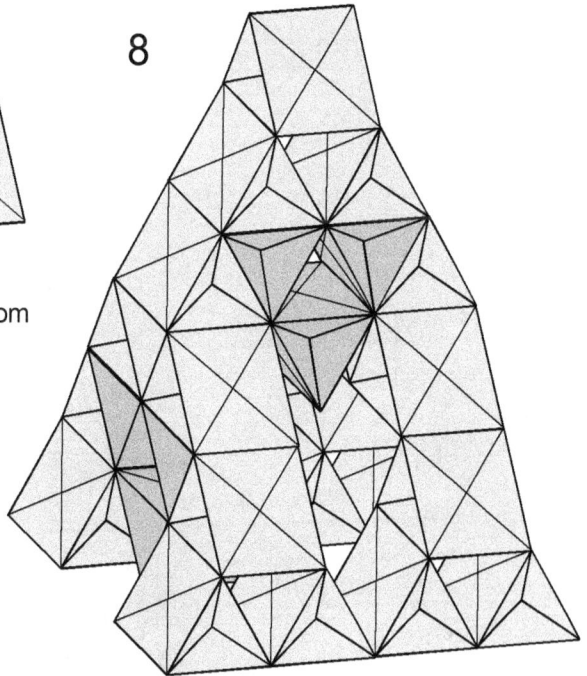

8. In larger structures, however, the bottom points of some of the inverted Alpha Pyramids will be left unsupported. This suggested the name of Damocles for this sculpture.

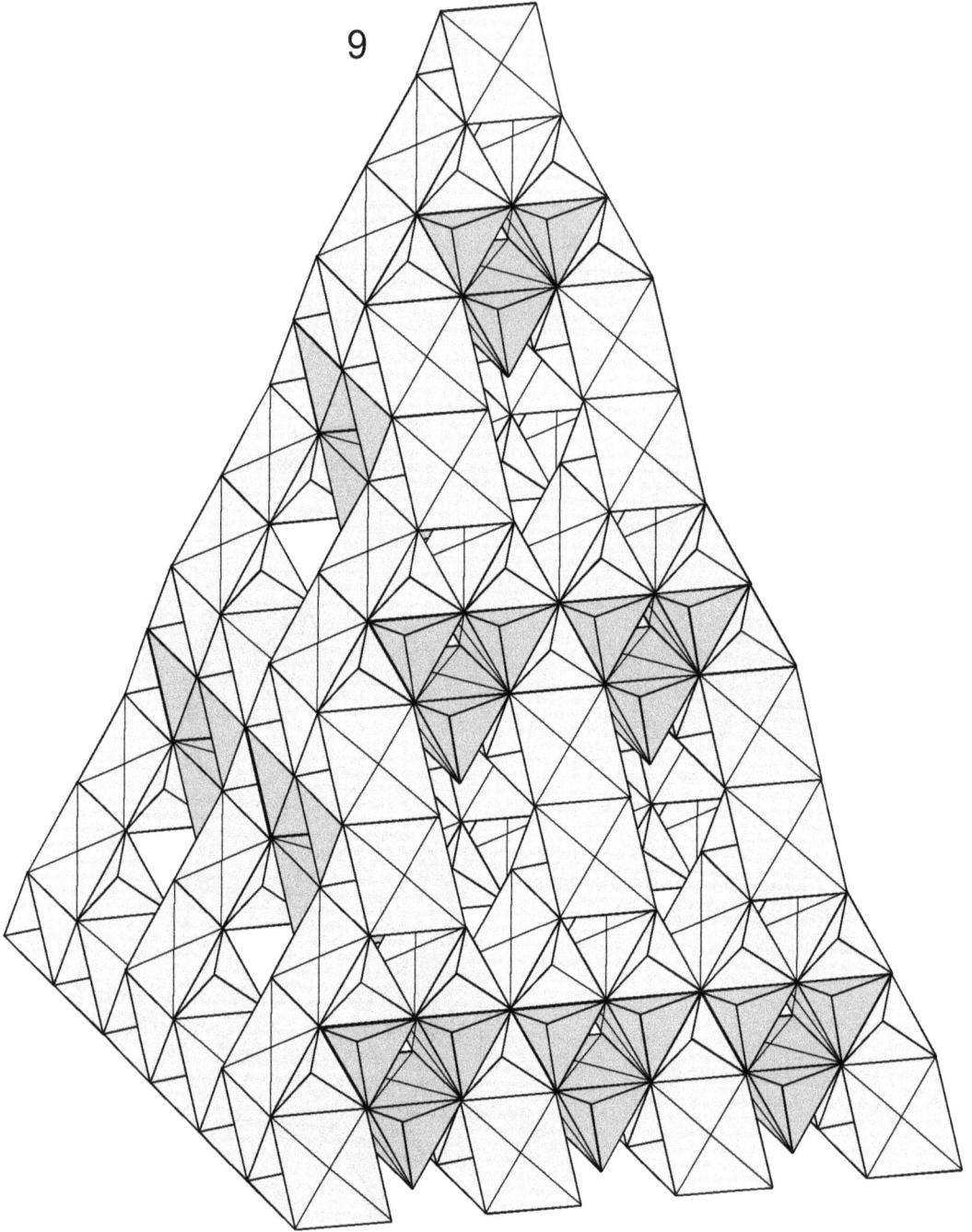

9

David Mitchell / Building with Butterflies

Treesnake

Diamond Prisms can be combined to produce sculptures resembling trees or snakes or, indeed, Treesnakes.

1

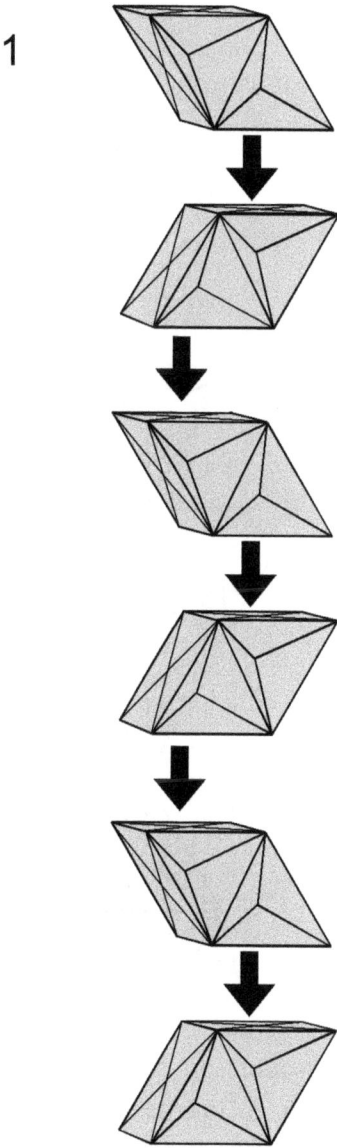

2

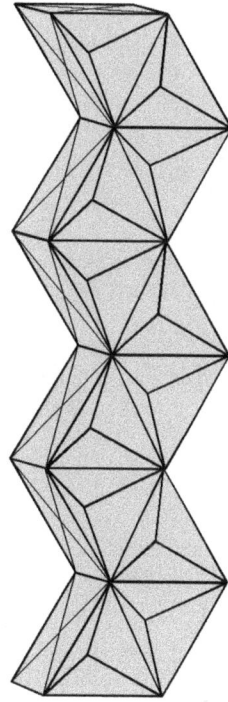

2. The result is stable if made from heavy paper or light card.

3

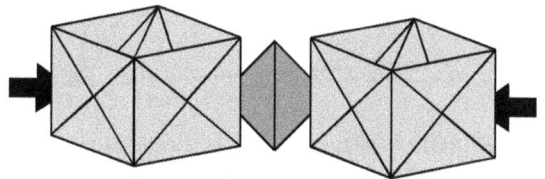

1. The simplest way to create a sculpture from Diamond Prisms is simply to stack them on top of each other like this.

3. Diamond Prisms can also be linked together into a chain using either of the methods used to link Alpha Prisms into pyramids.

4

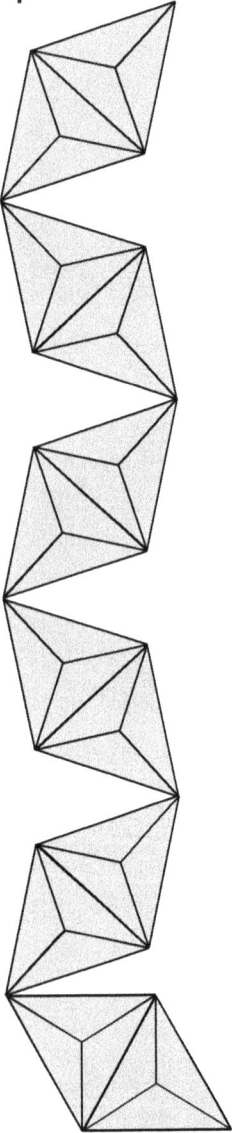

5

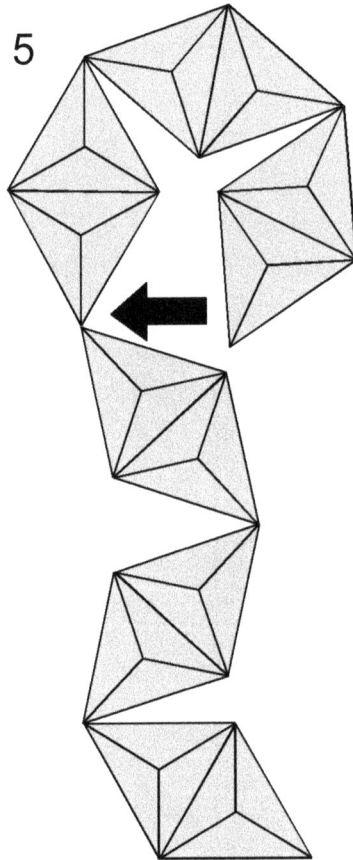

6

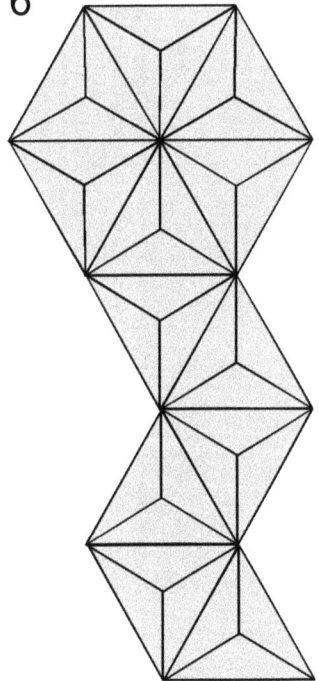

4. A chain of six Diamond Prisms will form a vertical snake sculpture of the kind shown in picture 2.

5. Alternatively, the top three prisms can be curled around ...

6. ... to create a tree-like sculpture. The designs on this page will work best when made from fairly lightweight paper.

Helterskelter

Gamma Antiprisms can be stacked to create Helterskelter, an intriguing sculpture on which the eye can dwell for hours without fully comprehending the clean complexity of the form.

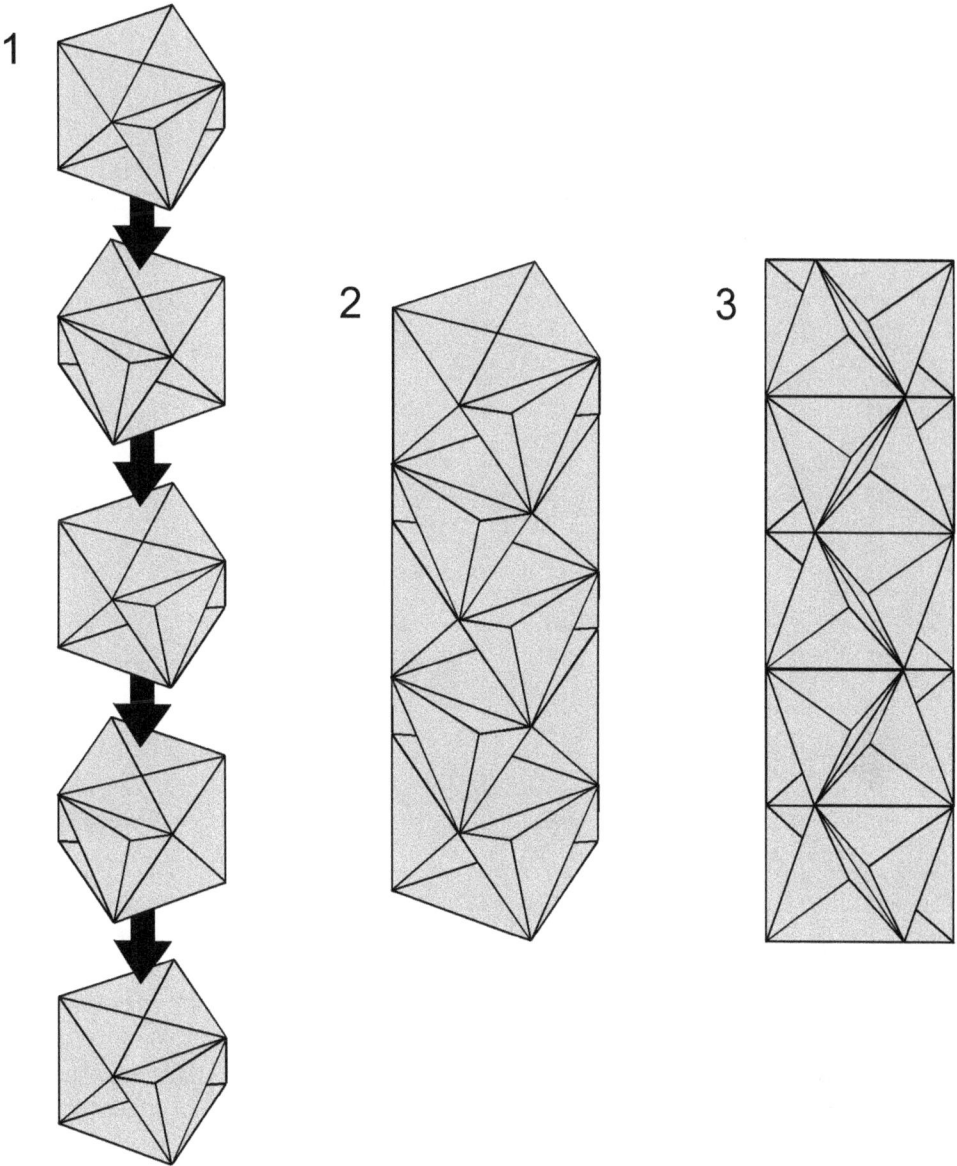

The Octahedral Tower

The Octahedral Tower is created by stacking Robert Neale's Octahedra and hexahedra in alternating layers. You can use Zeta Hexahedra to do this but it is more efficient of paper, and the result is better, if you use the link unit from the Columbus Pyramid (see pages 63 and 64). The link units will not be visible once the tower is complete.

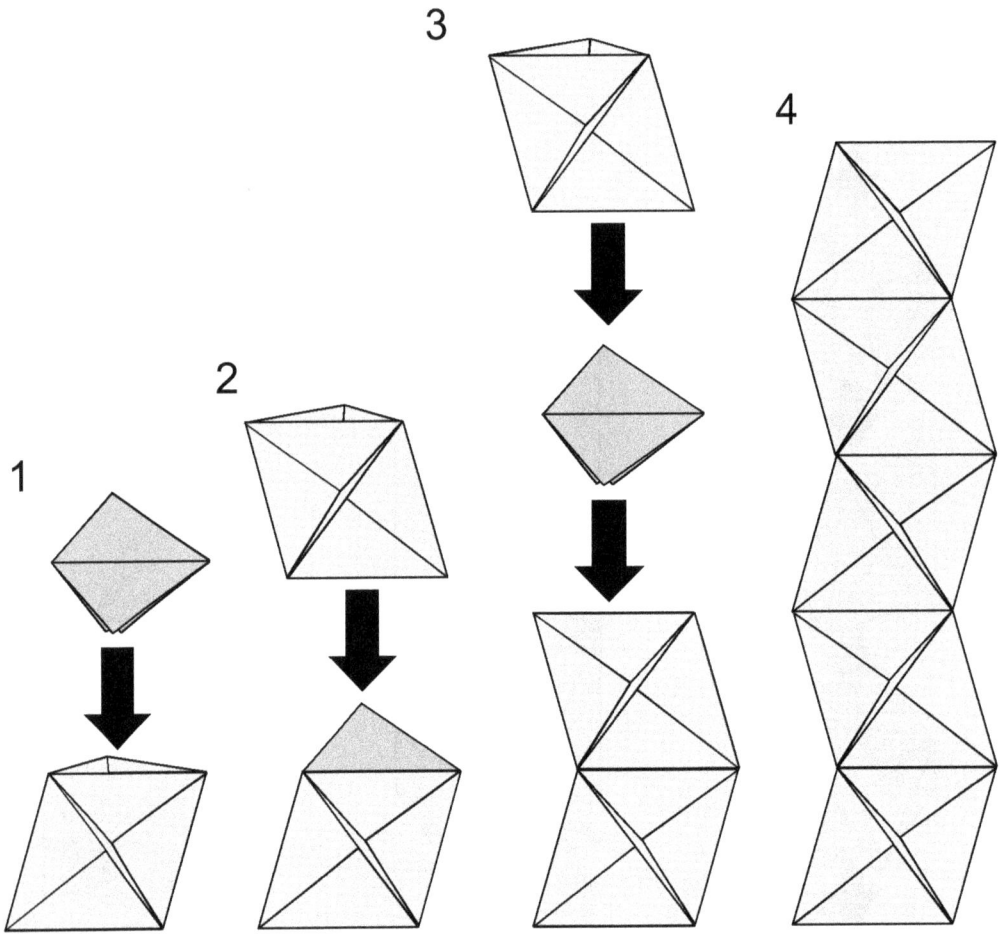

1. The open base of the link unit fits into the top of the first octahedron.

2. The second octahedron then drops on top of the link unit.

3. Continue adding link units and octahedra until the tower is complete.

4. When it is finished the Octahedral Tower will look like this.

David Mitchell / Building with Butterflies

The Octahedral Pyramid

The Octahedral Pyramid is also made by stacking Robert Neale's Octahedra with the help of a link unit, but in this case the tiers of the stack are offset so that a pyramid is formed. The link units not only provide a foundation for the tier above but also hold the tier below together.

Folding the link units

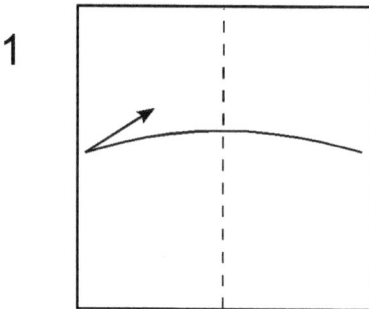

1

1. Fold in half sideways, then unfold.

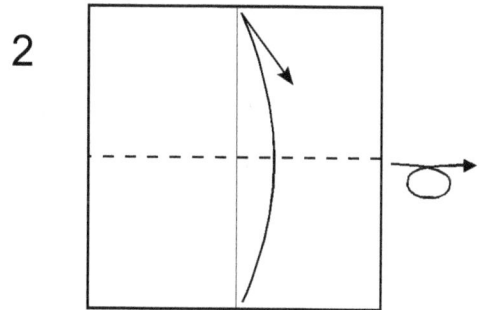

2

2. Fold in half upwards, then unfold. Turn over sideways.

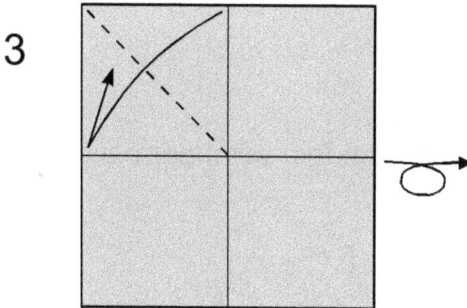

3

3. Make a crease along half of one diagonal. Turn over sideways again.

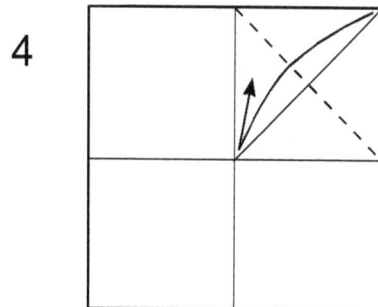

4

4. Fold the top right corner into the centre, then unfold.

5

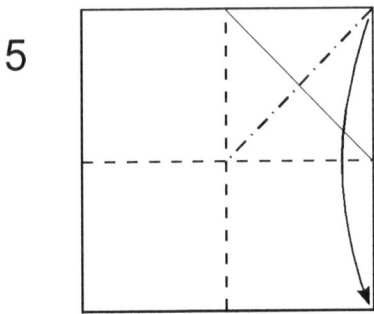

5. Fold the top right corner onto the bottom right corner. The design becomes three dimensional at this stage.

6

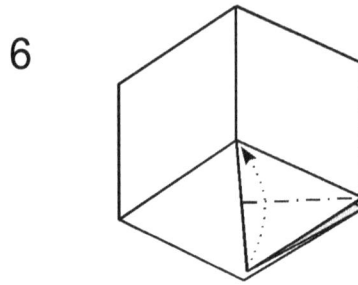

6. Fold the internal flap in half underneath itself to lock the folds in place.

7

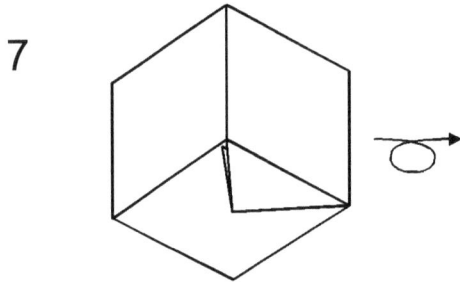

7. Turn over and arrange to look like picture 8.

8

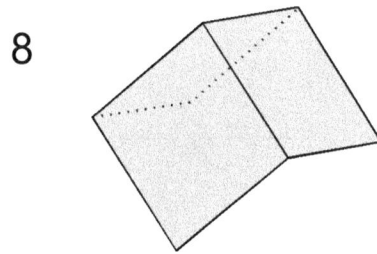

8. The link unit is finished.

Building the pyramids

The smallest Octahedral Pyramid is made from four octahedra and one link unit.

9

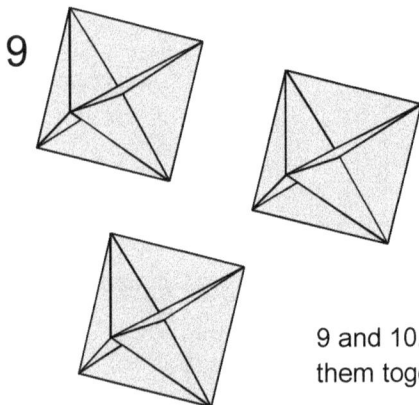

10

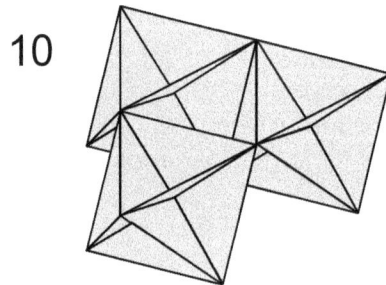

9 and 10. Lay three octahedra on a flat surface and bring them together so that the edges are aligned like this.

11

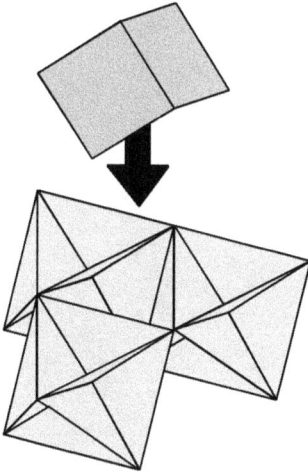

11. Place the link unit on top of the centre of the arrangement.

12

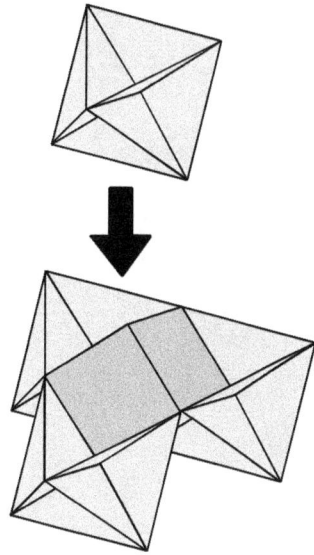

12. Add a fourth octahedron on top of the link unit.

13

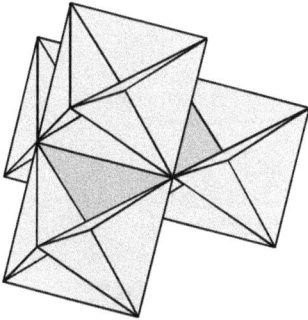

13. This is the smallest Octahedral Pyramid. It can be viewed as the product of six intersecting planes in the shape of 2x1 rectangles. Unfortunately, it isn't possible to pick out each of the planes in a separate colour using this modular method, since part of the link unit is visible in the centre of some of the faces.

14

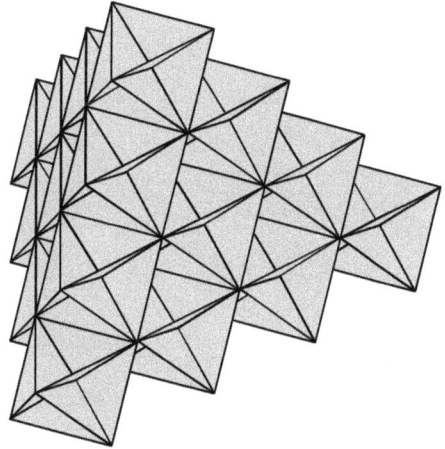

14. Larger Octahedral Pyramids can be built in a similar way. The next few pictures show you how to build a four tier pyramid. The design is robust and much larger pyramids are possible.

15

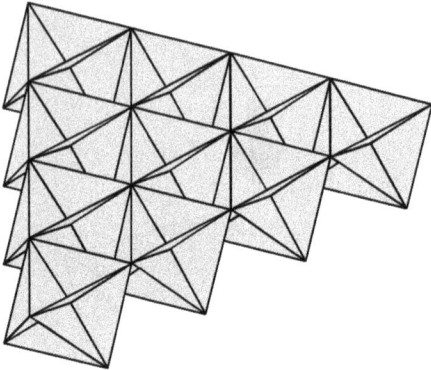

16

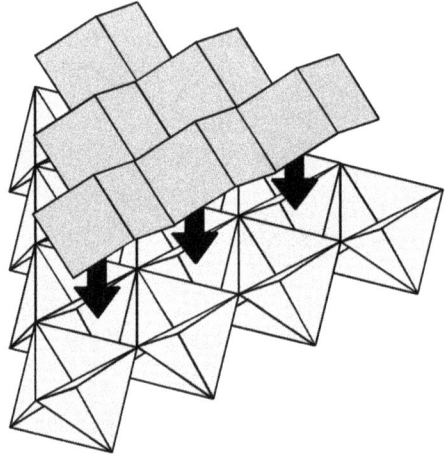

17

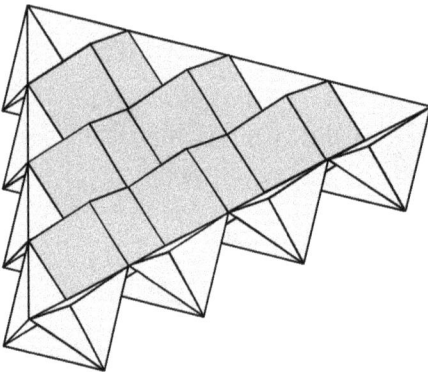

18

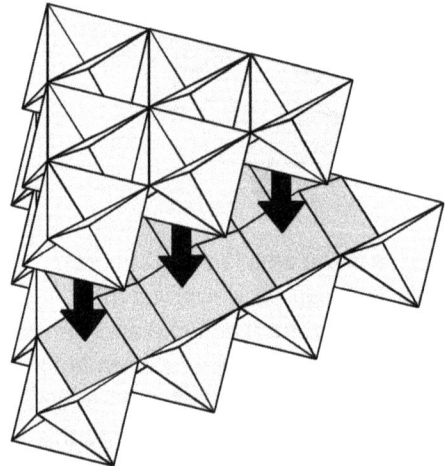

19

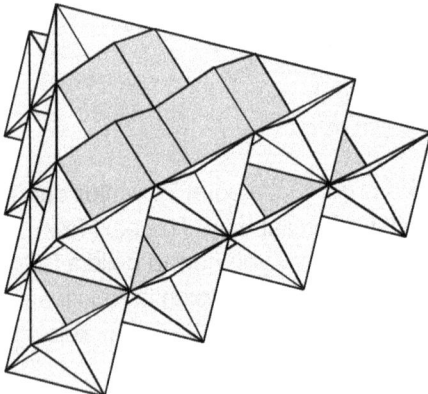

David Mitchell / Building with Butterflies

20

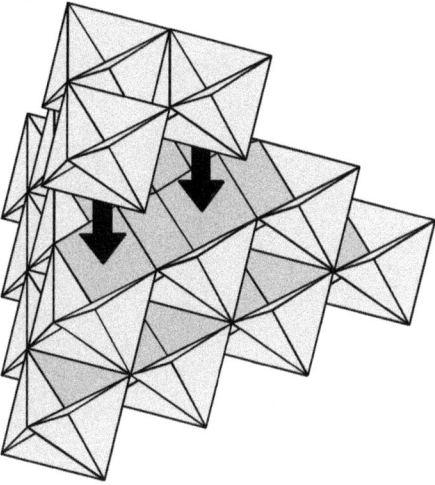

21

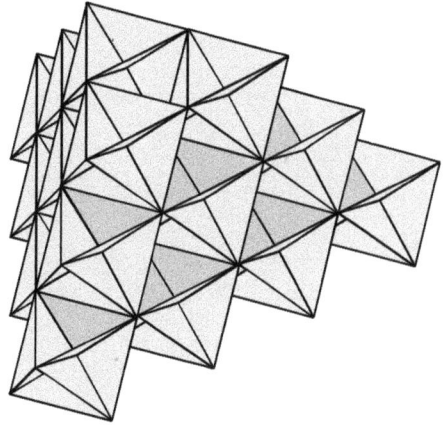

22

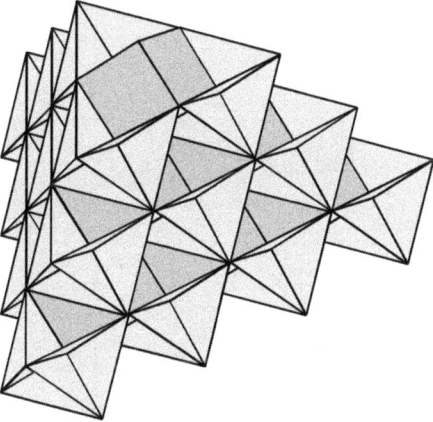

23

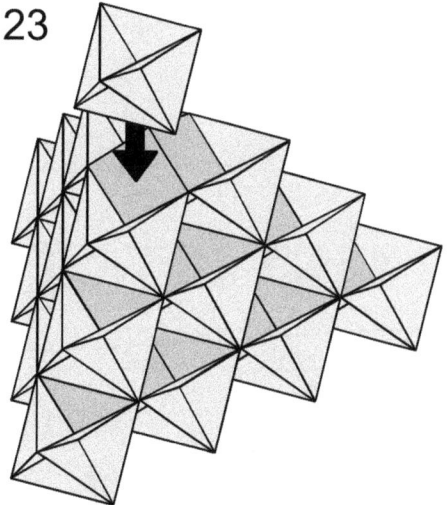

24

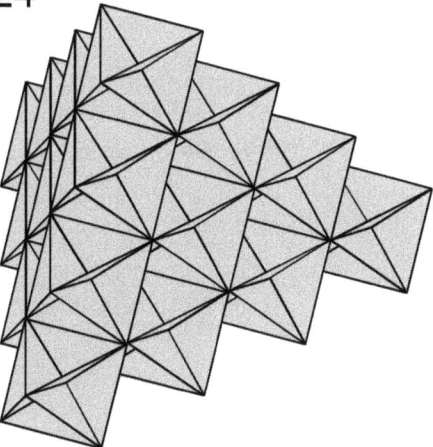

Combination
Sculptures

The Crooked Tower

Robert Neale's Octahedra and Paul Jackson's Cubes can be stacked together without using link units to create the Crooked Tower.

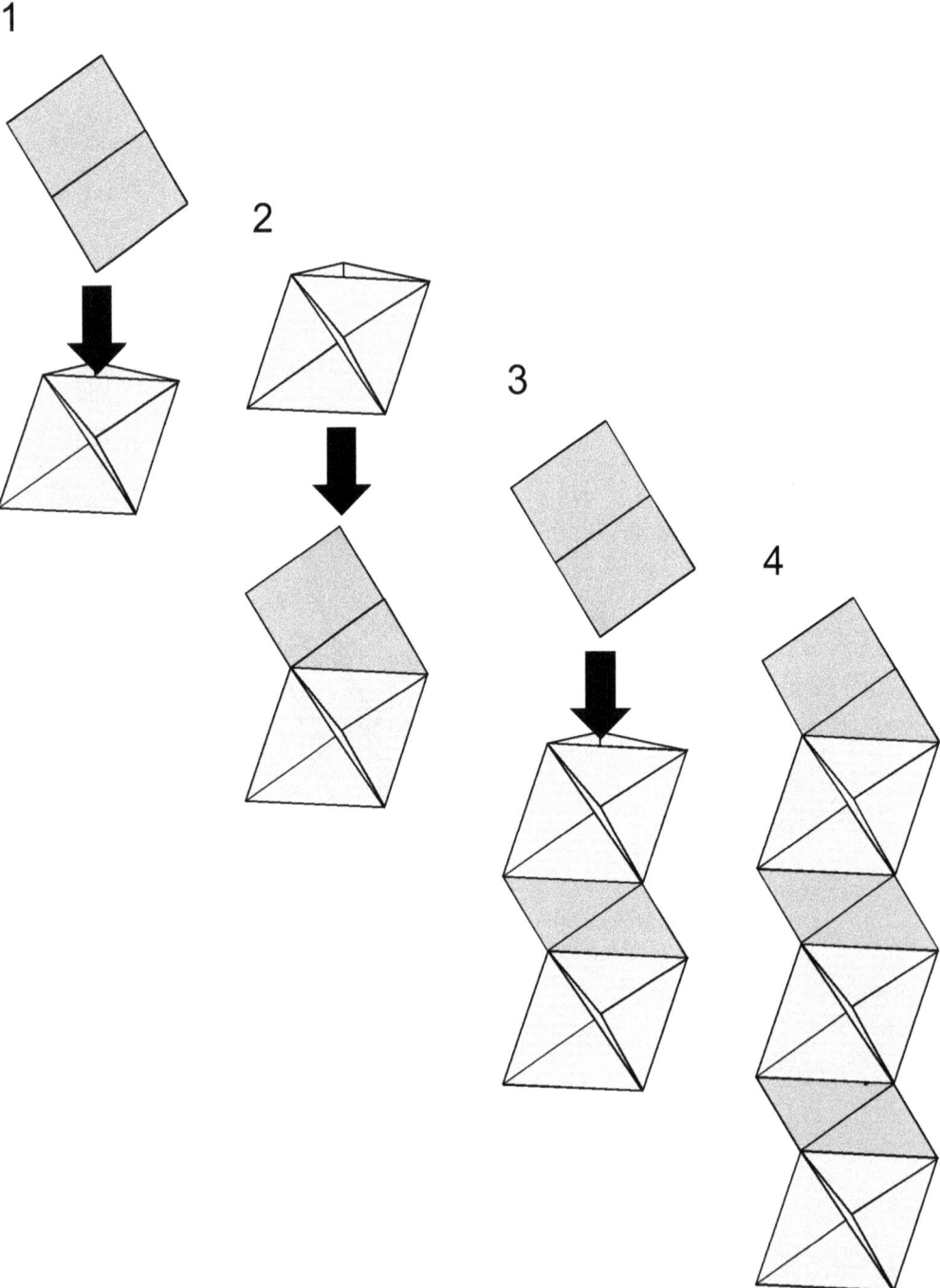

1

2

3

4

David Mitchell / Building with Butterflies

Tricorne

Tricorne is a distortion of the Zeta Hexahedron in which the top and bottom corners (those corners where the right angle corners of the faces meet) have been inverted. Tricorne is used as a macro-module to make the Leaning Tower and Slide.

If you are using irogami begin white side up.

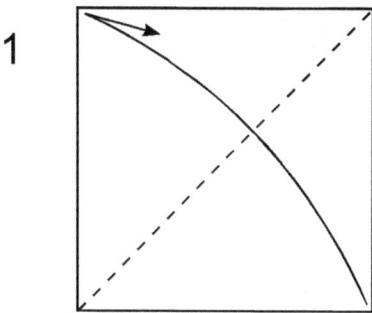

1

1. Fold in half diagonally, then unfold.

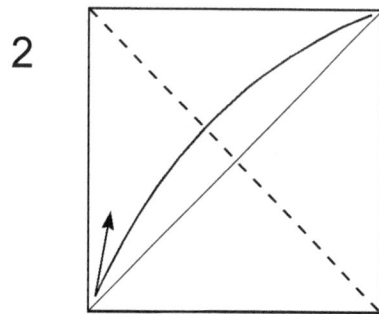

2

2. Fold in half diagonally in the other direction, then unfold.

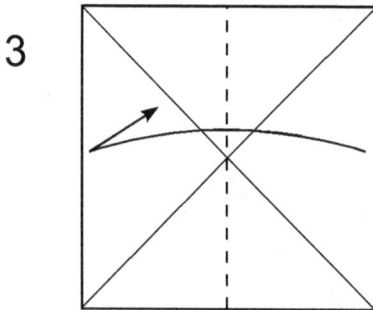

3

3. Fold in half sideways, then unfold.

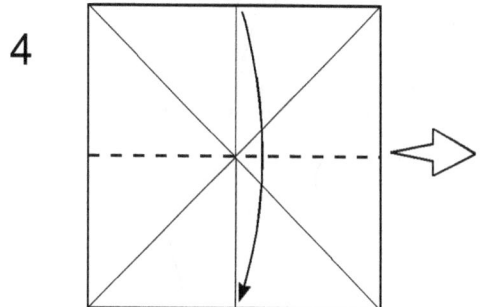

4

4. Fold in half downwards.

5

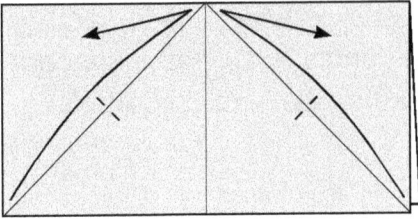

5. Make tiny creases across both diagonals to mark the half way points. You only need to make these creases in the front layer.

6

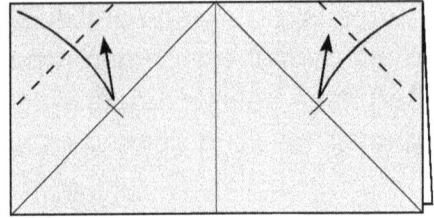

6. Fold both top corners inwards, using the point where the diagonal creases and the tiny creases made in step 5 intersect to locate the folds, then unfold.

7

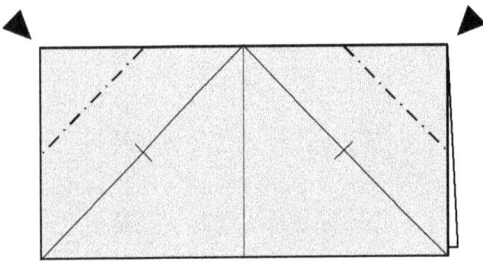

7. Turn both top corners inside out between the layers. You will need to reverse the direction of the creases made in the front layer in step 6 to achieve this.

8

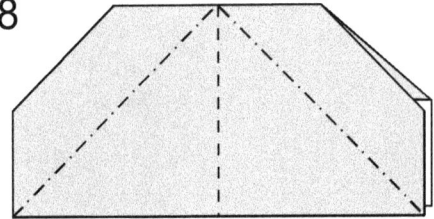

8. Configure the module so that it looks like picture 9.

9

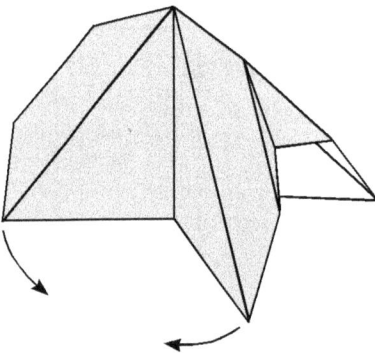

9. Continue configuring the module until it looks like picture 10.

10

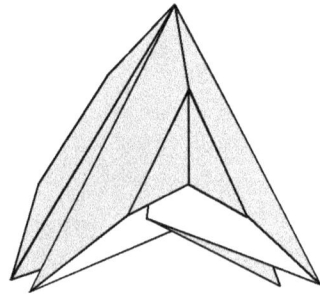

10. The Tricorne module is finished. Make three.

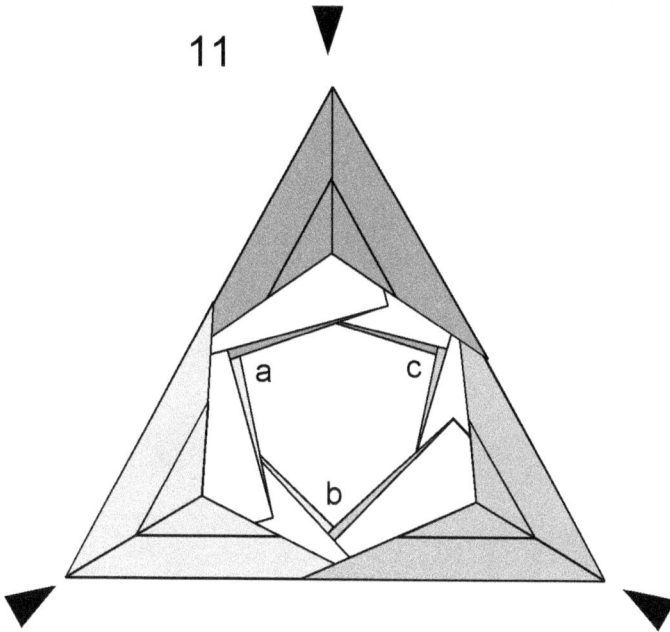

11

11. Tricorne is assembled in the same way as the Zeta Hexahedron (see page 100). After interweaving the arms, but before pushing the modules together, make sure the internal flaps are arranged like this. The set of flaps marked a push together in front, the set marked c go at the back and the set marked b lie in the middle.

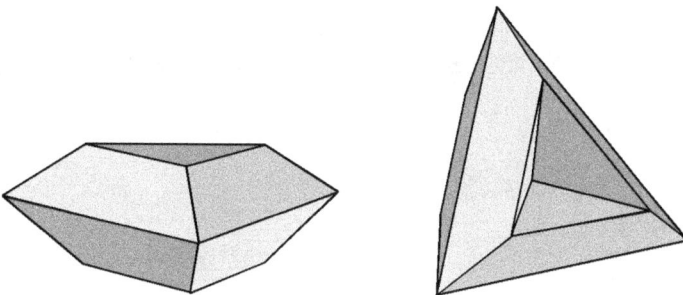

12

12. When finished, Tricorne will look like this. It is a very robust assembly.

The Leaning Tower

Paul Jackson's Cubes and Tricorne macro-modules will stack together to form the Leaning Tower. When seen from the right angle the Leaning Tower does indeed appear to lean, but this is just an illusion, of course.

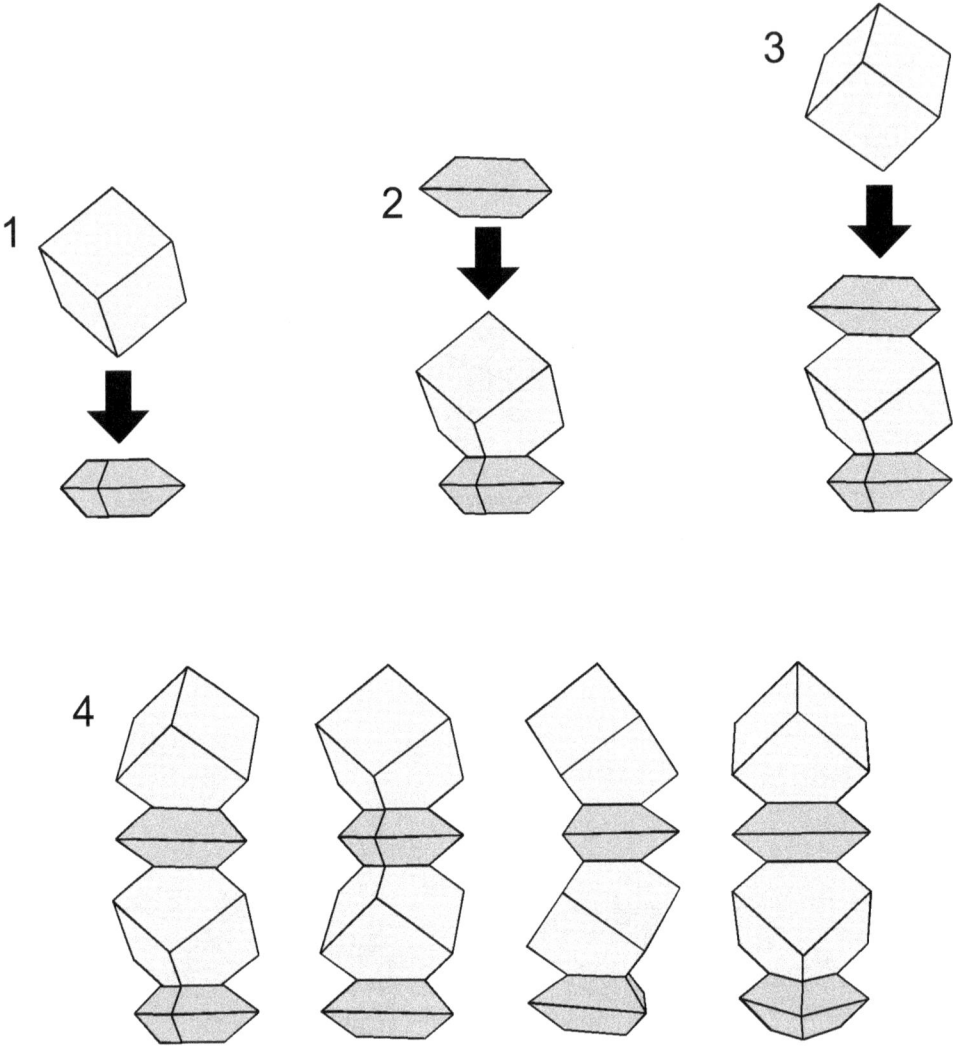

4. The illusion can be seen in the second picture from the right.

David Mitchell / Building with Butterflies

Slide

Slide is a development of the Columbus Pyramid which combines Columbus Cubes, Paul Jackson's Cubes, and Tricorne macro-modules into one stunning sculpture. In its original version, Slide was a variation of the Columbus Pyramid in which the link units were replaced by Tricorne macro-modules to let light inside the sculpture. I then found that if the cubes in each tier were not joined together I could separate them and allow the joining pieces linking them to the Tricorne macro-modules to slide (hence the name) down the pockets to allow the development of an entirely new form. The diagrams show you how to make a seven tier version of Slide.

1

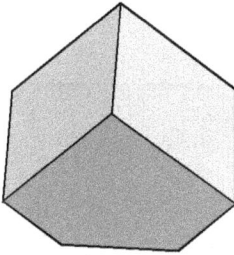

1. The base layer of the sculpture is composed of Columbus Cubes. A seven tier sculpture will have a base layer composed of ten Columbus Cubes.

2

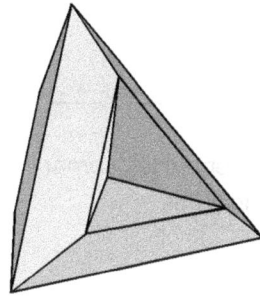

2. Each tier of cubes (except the top one) supports a tier of Tricorne macro-modules. The Tricorne macro-modules are linked to the tier of cubes below them using simple joining pieces. Ten Tricorne macro-modules are needed for a seven tier sculpture.

3

3. A tier of Paul Jackson's Cubes sits on top of each tier of Tricorne macro-modules. Ten cubes are required for a seven layer sculpture.

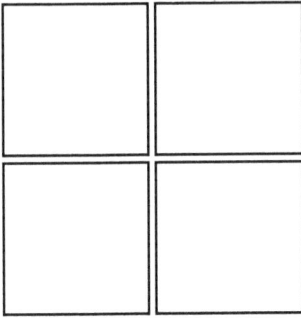

4. The joining pieces are made from squares one quarter the size of the squares used to fold the Tricorne macro-modules from.

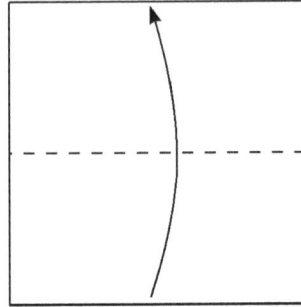

5. Fold in half upwards.

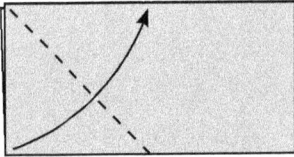

6. Fold the bottom left corner diagonally inwards.

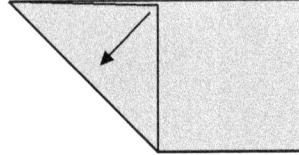

7. Open out the front flap so that the joining piece looks like picture 8.

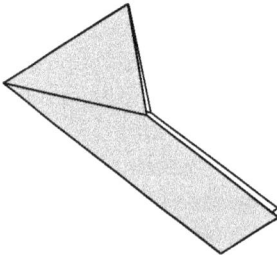

8. The joining piece is finished. Thirty joining pieces are required for a seven tier sculpture, three for each Tricorne macro-module.

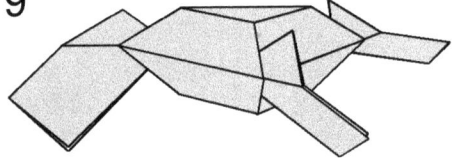

9. Insert three joining pieces inside the pockets to be found at the corners of a Tricorne macro-module like this.

David Mitchell / Building with Butterflies

10

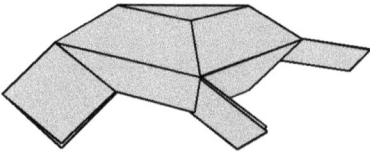

10. The first Tricorne sub-assembly is complete.

11

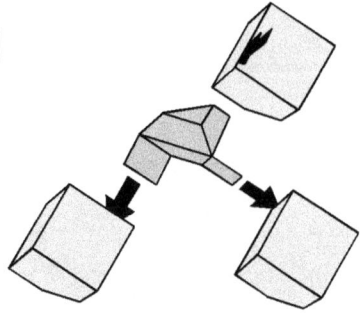

11. Insert the joining pieces into the pockets along the edges of three Columbus Cubes.

12

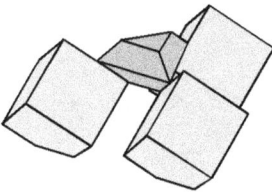

12. Move the cubes apart so that the joining pieces slide to the bottom of the pockets.

13

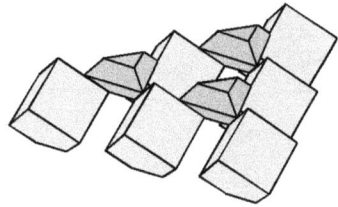

13. Add a row of three more Columbus Cubes to the base layer, using two further Tricorne sub-assemblies to link them together.

14

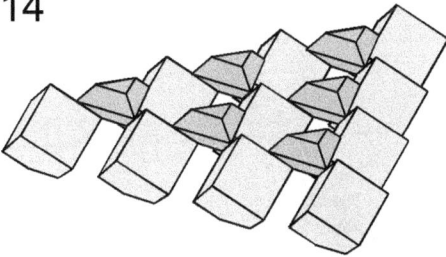

14. Add another row of four Columbus cubes and three Tricorne sub-assemblies. Make sure the edges of all the cubes are lined up with each other.

15

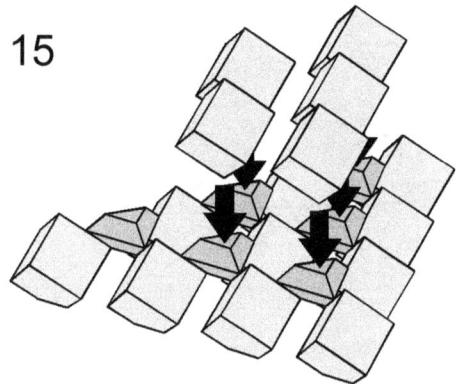

15. Five Paul Jackson's Cubes sit on top of the Tricorne sub-assemblies.

16

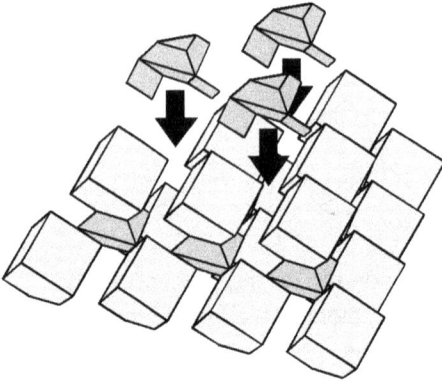

16. Three Tricorne sub-assemblies hold the cubes in place.

17

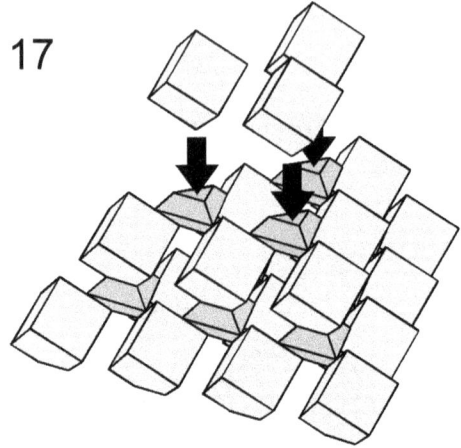

17. Add another layer of cubes ...

18

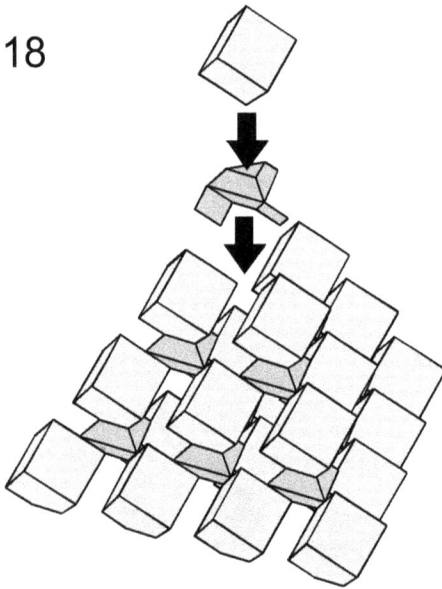

18. ... which are held in place by the last Tricorne sub-assembly ... and finally drop the last cube on top.

19

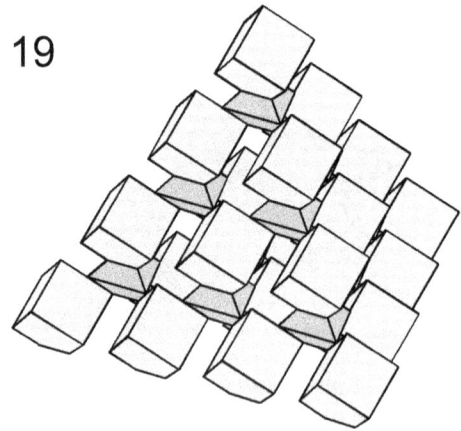

19. Slide is finished.

David Mitchell / Building with Butterflies

And Finally

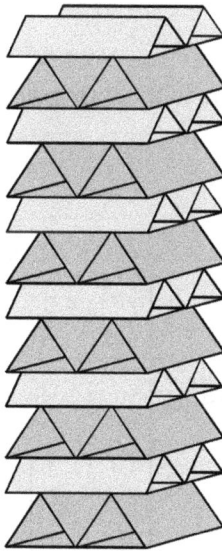

Tokyo Towers

Tokyo Towers are built from two sets of triangular section tubes, one long and one short. There are various ways to combine these tubes to build Tokyo Towers, some easier than others.

The diagrams show you how to fold the two kinds of tubes from A4 paper. The advantage of using this shape is that the area covered by two long tubes and by two fat tubes is the same, which means that the outside edges of the towers line up rather neatly. The design will still work if you use a rectangle of different proportions, for instance US letter size paper, but the final result will be slightly less neat. If you use squares the edges will line up neatly, but all the tubes will be the same size. The choice is yours.

If you are using irogami begin with your paper arranged white side up.

Folding the long tubes

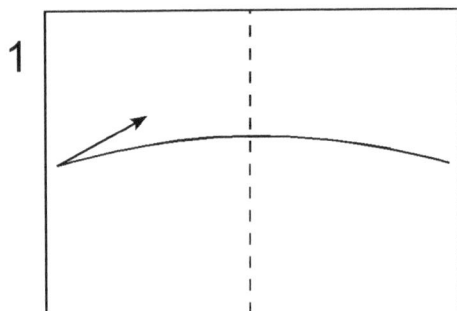

1. Fold in half from right to left, then unfold.

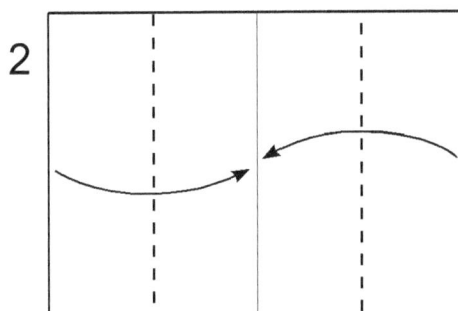

2. Fold the left and right edges inwards to lie along the vertical centre crease, then unfold.

3

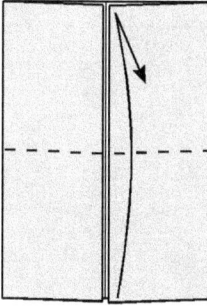

3. Fold in half from bottom to top, then unfold.

4

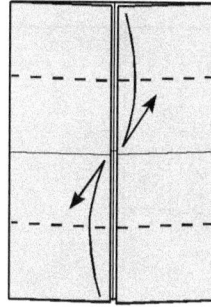

4. Fold the top and bottom edges inwards to lie along the horizontal centre crease, then unfold.

5

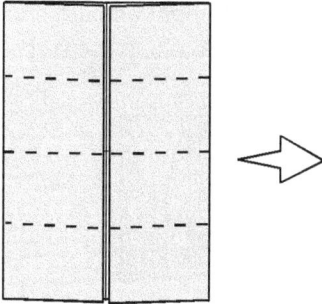

5. Use the creases made in steps 3 and 4 to fold the paper into the shape shown in picture 6.

6

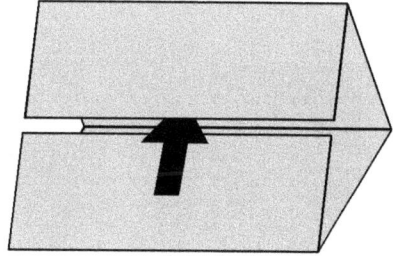

6. Begin to form the tube by inserting one end of the paper inside the other.

7

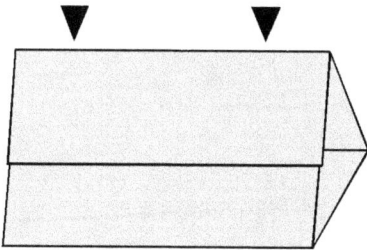

7. Lay the partly formed tube on a flat surface and apply gentle, even pressure on the top edge to persuade the two ends to slide completely inside each other.

8

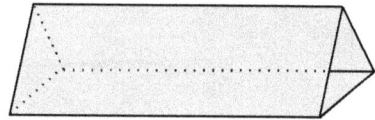

8. The first long tube is finished. When building the towers, long tubes are always used in pairs.

Folding the short tubes

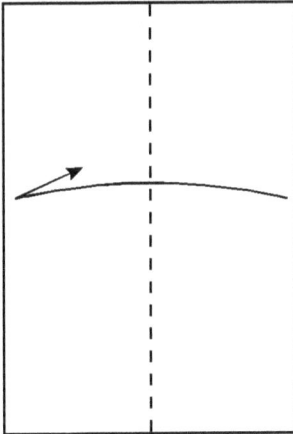

9. Fold in half from right to left, then unfold.

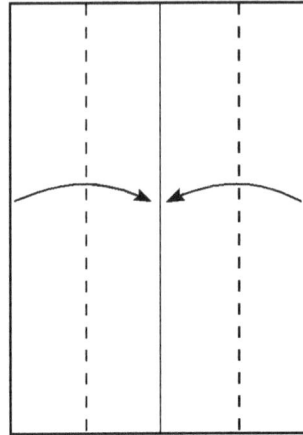

10. Fold the right and left hand edges inwards to lie along the vertical crease.

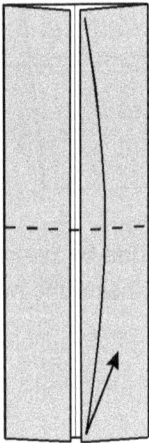

11. Fold in half from top to bottom, then unfold.

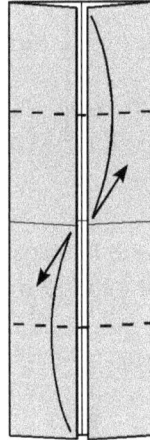

12. Fold the top and bottom edges inwards to lie along the horizontal centre crease, then unfold.

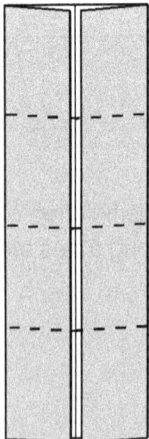

13. Use the creases made in steps 11 and 12 to fold the paper into the form shown in picture 14.

14. Begin forming the tube by inserting one end of the paper inside the other.

David Mitchell / Building with Butterflies

15

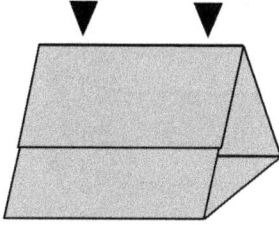

15. Lay the partly formed tube on a flat surface and apply gentle, even pressure on the top edge to persuade the two ends to slide completely inside each other.

16

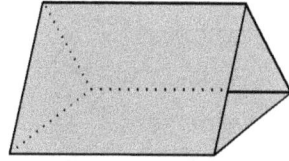

16. The first short tube is finished. When building the towers, short tubes are also always used in pairs.

Building the Tokyo Towers

17

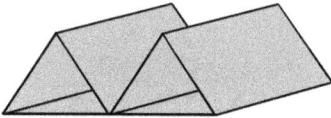

17. Arrange two short tubes side by side.

18

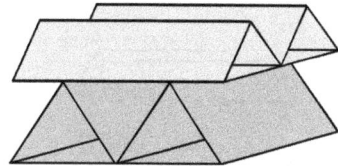

18. Lay two long tubes across them so that the edges of the layers are aligned vertically.

19

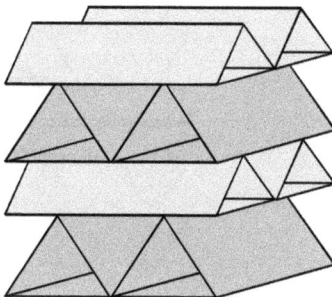

19. Add alternate layers of short and long tubes to build up the layers of the tower.

20

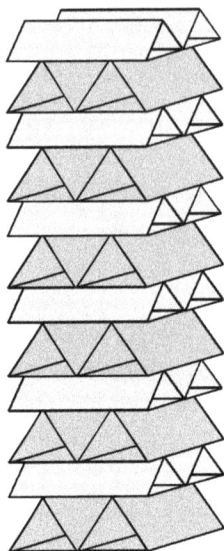

20. The first Tokyo Tower is finished. This one is easy.

21

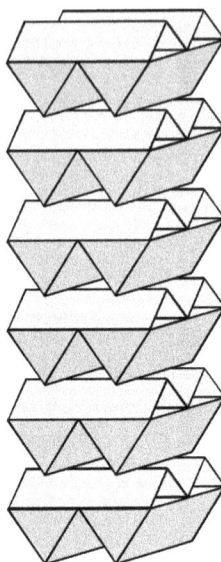

21. This one is more difficult.

22

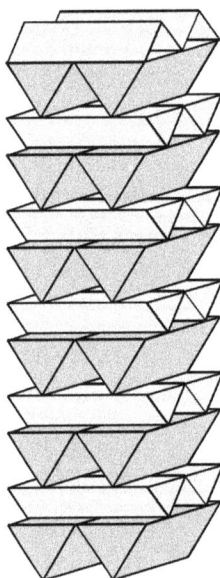

22. This one is more difficult still (especially for just one person).

23

23. And this one is possibly quite impossible. Try it and see.

www.ingramcontent.com/pod-product-compliance
Lightning Source LLC
Chambersburg PA
CBHW062046090426

42740CB00016B/3038